*Skelligs Calling*

*Cliathán na Sceilge*, 1984
*Tochtar Trá*, 1985
*An Gabhar sa Teampall*, 1986
*Barra Taoide*, 1988
*Ríocht na dTonn*, 1989
*Ceol Maidí Rámha*, 1990
*Skelligside*, 1990
*Iníon Keevac*, 1996
*Guth ón Sceilg*, 2000

# *Skelligs Calling*

## Michael Kirby

*Michael Kirby* (signature)

THE LILLIPUT PRESS
DUBLIN

First published 2003 by
THE LILLIPUT PRESS LTD
62–63 Sitric Road, Arbour Hill,
Dublin 7, Ireland
www.lilliputpress.ie

A CIP record for this title is available
from The British Library.


10 9 8 7 6 5 4 3 2 1


ISBN 1 84351 026 X

Photographs within the text are courtesy of
Fionán O'Connell / Crosslight Photography

The Lilliput Press receives financial assistance from
An Chomhairle Ealaíon / The Arts Council of Ireland.


Set in 12.5 on 15 Adobe Garamond by Marsha Swan
Printed in Ireland by ßetaprint of Dublin

*Do mo bhean chéile Peig is dom chlann uilig*

For my wife Peggy and my family

# Contents

# FOREWORD

What a pleasure it is to read this wonderful collection of memories and reflections, fact, folklore, and natural history, written by the magical and multifaceted Michael Kirby in the tenth decade of his life. Poet, painter, and fisherman, writer and raconteur, Irish speaker and prodigious reader, Kirby is a man of stately physical bearing and wide ranging mental activity. There is nothing too large or too small to be kept in the house of his mind, no square inch of the perceived world that has escaped his attention and his terrific curiosity. And his imagist's eye and lyrical sensibility lends a natural cadence to the subjects he explores, almost as if his stories are sung rather than told.

Kirby is a man who both knows and loves his 'place'; that rough patch of sea, sand, rock, fern and heather where he has lived his long and rich life. The place in question is Ballinskelligs, County Kerry, Ireland: the beautiful Ballinskelligs Bay, and the waters that move away from it, past Bolus Head, and out toward the mystical Skellig Islands. In this book he invites us to accompany him on a journey that will make us intimate with the region's coastline and headlands, its islands and its beautifully named ancient sites.

But this is no ordinary voyage. Kirby has spent his life learning the rhythms of sea and coastal life, and he is eager to share his wisdom with the reader. We are encouraged to explore caves that can only be seen from the water, to listen to the various cries of birds – some who speak Irish – to come to know 'Rónán' the seal who guards the mouth of the harbour. We are told of night rainbows, of an open cottage door that is used as a sundial and of a thorn bush that is used as a chimney sweep. We are taught how to listen to the voices of the various strands, how to read the ever-changing sky, how to gut fish and how amazing surprises can spill from these guts. We are permitted entrance to the inner life of a poet and fisherman who is bidding farewell to his boat.

Michael Kirby is a man who understands the true value of life, marine life to be certain, but also life in the larger sense. He shows us in this marvellous book that everything that lives is indeed connected, that to fail to honour the smallest blade of grass is to fail to honour the earth itself and everything that walks, swims, grows or flies on, under, or around its surface. His is the view of the wise man who has cherished his life from its earliest days to the quieter times of advanced age, and has found great joy in engaging with his surroundings. We have much to learn from him.

Jane Urquhart
*Stratford, Ontario, Canada*
*Coshcummeragh, Mastergeehy, County Kerry*

# PREFACE

During World War Two, the Morse-code signalling with lamps and flags became history. With the advent of the radio-telephone, light-keepers were able to communicate with passing ships, the life-saving station and their home base, also at Valentia. It was only a matter of dialling a code number and repeating 'Skelligs Calling' into the receiver. All lighthouses were equipped with radio- telephone and each had a different code number. I had the honour of knowing several wonderful men stationed on Skellig Michael. One was Michael Smith and another was Dick Coughlan. They were kindly and affable, devoid of any false vanity, tending the beacon's warning flash to bring hope to many a weary mariner guiding his craft through the maelstrom of a violent sea or the serenity of calm.

My grandparents' holding was close to that of the monastic settlement, built by the monks of Skelligs, who had been forced to flee from the plundering Northmen and pillaging Vikings and seek the security of the mainland. Thus the monastery gave its name to my townland, *Baile 'n Sceilg* – 'Ballinskelligs'.

History and folklore instilled in me an ardent desire to learn more about the natural habitat and environs that the monks of Skellig Michael were forced to vacate. From my teenage years onwards I availed of every opportunity to sense the aura pervading this wild citadel of the seabound sanctuary. During the summer and autumn lobster-fishing season maybe I too heard Skelligs calling, eating crab claws and drinking mugs of tea while rocked in my chariot, listening to the raucous chorus of what we rudely term 'wild creatures'.

## Skelligs Calling

One fine soft morning
And Skelligs calling
Our boat sped fleetly
Across the bay,
With Father Dermot
On the thwart beside me
Our hearts were light
In the sunshine ray.

It was his intention
I now will mention
Christ's loving Mass
On the rock to pray,
Our oarsman willing
And canvas filling,
Our craft was leaping
In the surging spray.

*Skelligs Calling*

# I

## *Fish, Fishing and the Life of a Fisherman*

# EARLY SEA MEMORIES

My father, John Kirby, kept a small boat down near the old ruined castle, which to this day stands on the beach in the town land of Ballinskelligs. The boat was built locally, of carvel design, from native timber, only twenty feet long overall, and five feet ten inches beam, propelled by oars and a small sail of old rough linen resembling sackcloth. The local builder swore by the Book that each and every boat built by his hands would contain three special qualities which he described in Irish as *siúl, iompar agus cosaint*, meaning 'speed, cargo capacity and resistance to a rough sea'. Old Johnny Morty Galvin from *Brácathrach* was proud of his skill; his was the *modus operandi*, the knack and the know-how of his time. Therefore my father's boat became our family's most sacrosanct item of property, and small wonder, for it provided a goodly supply of prime fish, which helped us to survive within a lean and meagre period in our economy. It is neither my intention nor my wish to write a history bewailing the lot of those who survived the Great Famine, and who were yet only one step away from the coffin ships or morsels from a landlord's table.

Now, up until my eighth birthday, I had not yet seen the boat. I was prohibited from straying too far from the scene of my delivery. It never occurred to me that I was being a good boy, and I had heard that the boy Jesus went down to Nazareth and was subject to his parents, to grow in wisdom and understanding, traits I confess I have never fully achieved. I had heard of the word 'curfew', which for me at any rate meant that I stay indoors, say my bedtime prayers and go to bed.

Then one day something utterly surprising happened. The curfew was lifted. A milestone, which to this day stands out clearly in my mind, my father saying, 'We're going fishing – tell Mam get your boots and jacket.'

I had only one pair of boots, rough boots, complete with heavy iron tips and hobnails. I was allowed to wear them once a week to attend Sunday Mass, and maybe some special occasion like the 'Pattern' day – the remainder of the week it was God's leather to God's weather. Oh, but this was a special occasion; my dad had lifted the curfew, he had invited me into his workplace, that vast kingdom below high-water mark where

*They don't plant taters*
*And don't plant cotton.*

That evening perhaps my father knew he was about to foster in me a lasting permanent love for my native surroundings, which in so many ways would influence my development and behaviour for years to come. This coupled with my eager drive to know more about the strange and fascinating secrets of nature, some of which are beyond our capacity to understand. This is the workplace that my dad introduced me to, that of a small-time fisherman. This is the kingdom I would feign have the temerity to understand, much less to write about. That fishing trip was the commencement of a way of life, which culminated in thirty years involvement with the sea.

I will only vouch for what I have observed from my own personal experience. The picture which I try to lay before you, is only an attempt at describing an immense, beautiful world of water and wave, towering cliff, crag and cave, sand and seashore, green islands, barren rock, pebble beaches and silver strands.

This is Neptune's territory, Mannanán's Kingdom, containing fin, fur and feather. Its many gardens show a manifold array of marine plants, each with diverse mineral content, most having curative healing powers beneficial to man and beast. A rock pool can become an Aladdin's Cave, teeming with multi-species of life, from the microscopic organism to the pearl oyster.

It is my intention to describe as far as possible the habits and lifestyles of some different bird families, those beautiful creatures I became familiar with during my life as a fisherman.

Weather signs of other days, which clash with modern technology, make interesting reading; shellfish, marine plants and animals, are all part and parcel of a

> *Life on the ocean wave,*
> *And a home on the rolling deep*
> *Where scattered waters rave*
> *And winds their revels keep.*

I am not familiar with the Latin names of my marine species – my Latin happens to be Irish. To all you good people, both ornithologists and scientists, I crave your pardon. If I have become a fly in your ointment, please let me off the hook.

## Sea Tears

*Why have I forgotten?*
*Things that dreams*
*Are made from*
*A white sail*
*The harbour lights*
*The little footprints*
*On the sands*
*Were mine.*

*Little white waves*
*Played chase with me,*
*Laughing, splashing,*
*Ebbing and flowing,*
*Catching up with me*
*Drowning my legs*
*Leaving me*
*Sighing, gasping, exhausted.*

*My thoughts now*
*Like a troubled ocean*
*The tempest of life*
*Make dim the harbour lights,*
*Her wild horses*
*Beat thunder in my ears,*
*Frothing, fuming, filling*
*Deep caverns*
*Of my ageing years.*
*Pounding, surging, swirling,*
*Playing chase once more,*
*Washing the memory*
*Of little footprints*
*With her salty tears.*

# A FISHERMAN LOVES HIS BOAT

If I write about birds, rocks, sea, sharks and seaweed, I feel I must also write about boats. Great ships have foundered and small boats have remained afloat. A fisherman loves his boat; he knows exactly what she is capable of in a rough seaway. Jim, our skipper, was like that. I would often hear him speak in low tones when taking her through a high breaking sea where green water could be seen towering at a level with her lifting bow. He would miraculously avoid the menacing hillock of water that seemed poised to crash aboard. A sudden flick of the helm would 'knock her away' to let the breaking sea pass harmlessly by starboard or port quarter. This trick might be repeated again and again until we entered sheltered waters.

On occasions such as this I often heard him give instructions to the helmsman. If he saw an extra dangerous sea he would say, 'Watch out for that one!' 'Turn her away quickly, beautiful!' 'Bring her up again!' 'Split the weather in the eye!' He would praise the boat that would climb and pull steadily in a heavy seaway: 'Over it old girl'. On the other hand he would call a sluggish boat a 'dirty bitch'. The boat is always feminine. Another type of boat would be referred to as 'a giddy little whore without enough gut', gut meaning width or beam. The jargon of a fisherman can be excessively salty at its best and at its worst unsuitable for the cloister or the early Victorian drawing-room.

Boats broad on the transom, and feminine-breasted lobster boats from Brest and Saint Malo, fished for crayfish off the Kerry coast. On board, wooden-clogged Breton sailors drank cask-fulls of dark, sour claret wine with every meal.

An old schooner from Brest called *Sea Thrift* came monthly to the South Kerry coast to buy and collect lobsters and crayfish for the French market. I loved to go on board, if only to smell the

Stockholm tar and the rich perfume of the ships that pass in the night. We called her captain *Mataí Leathchoise*. He wore a yellow, wooden peg-leg stump from the knee, complete with the ferrule and leather pad for use on deck. It was fascinating to watch this big middle-aged man stomp all over a slippery, rolling deck, as agile as a cat without ever a slip. He used a more modern artificial limb for special occasions when going ashore. A neighbour of mine, Michael Curran, 'Old Curran' as we called him, came of old fishing stock and always sold his lobsters to Mataí Peg-Leg. Michael often arrived late only to be berated by Captain Mataí, who would say, 'Why are you always coming aboard when I'm just about to turn in? I will be heaving my anchor at dawn. I'm an ordinary human who needs eight hours sleep.' Old Curran never made excuses or answered back, only hung his head and remained silent, whereupon the Frenchman would feel a little sorry and proffer him a jigger of cognac when paying him. His parting remark was, 'Do try and come a little earlier next time, Michael.' Curran would sing the praises of Captain Mataí na Leathchoise as a gentleman, *duine galánta.*

Michael's punt was only twelve feet long, carvel built, having only one seat amidships and one stern seat. It was known as the *Tar Pot*, because of annual applications of boiling tar over the years. Old Curran was an expert swimmer. In his declining years he never ventured far from the harbour reefs owing to his frail craft. He carried his lobster pots, eight at a time, and always had a bucket for bailing. He would say, 'I'm always ready to abandon my ship.' One day his words were put to the test. The *Tar Pot* sprang a leak close to Horse Island. Michael stuffed his jacket into the gaping hole, jettisoning all his lobster gear, and rowing as he never rowed in his life, pausing only momentarily to ply the bucket. He succeeded in staying afloat until finally he beached his stricken vessel on the shingle of Horse Island, where he was well-received by the Fitzgerald family, who instantly set to and repaired the damaged plank.

The great craft was once more declared seaworthy and in the words of the poet, 'Her timbers yet are sound, and she shall float again.' Old Curran put to sea once more on the evening tide, bringing to mind Tennyson's beautiful poem:

> *Sunset and the evening star,*
> *And one clear call for me!*
> *And may there be no moaning of the bar*
> *When I put out to sea.*
> *Twilight and evening bell*
> *And after that the dark!*
> *And may there be no sadness of farewell,*
> *When I embark.*

Many British steam trawlers found anchorage in Ballinskelligs Bay. It was a very convenient base for shelter owing to its close proximity to the rich fishing grounds on the Atlantic shelf off southwest Ireland, from Bantry Bay to Galway and south-westward to the Porcupine Bank. The sea in this area teamed with fish, which were of great commercial value. Big iron-hulled steamships replaced the wooden boats. They could work in very severe weather. The 'Castle Boats' worked out of Milford Haven and Swansea. Others came from as far apart as Aberdeen and Hull. Large Dutch trawlers, manned by English crews, enjoyed the rich pickings and rape of the Irish coast. Poaching was blatantly indulged in. The British authorities who were responsible for the conservation of Irish fish stocks and the fostering of the fishing industry in Ireland, turned a blind eye on fishing within the imaginary three mile limit, which in terms of legality was only a cruel joke. The fishing vessel used for the protection of the entire Irish coast, was an old tin can version of a gunboat, carrying a two-pounder gun mounted on the forecastle. This ship, called the *Helga,* was seldom at sea, and was used later in defence of the realm, being ordered to sail up the Liffey and quell the disorderly but successful Irish 'rabble' who dared challenge the might of the British empire. History tells us that the two-pounder was kept busy that morning, not adding greatly to the glory of a mighty empire.

I can remember names of ships like the *Thomas Booth, Isaac*

*Walton, Cleopatra, Dunraven Castle, Tenby Castle, Cardigan Castle, Princess Maria Jose, Princess Alexandria, Labore et Honore,* and a host of ships too numerous to mention here. Their skippers were tough old sea dogs who had only one motto in mind: keep the net in the water, and get the fish in the hold and, when ice and coal were low, run for the market, replenish the ships stores and it's back to the fishing grounds once more.

The crews were a mixture of different nationalities, all badly paid for the strenuous work and long hours they endured, but at least provided with good food and bunks, plus three pounds ten shillings per week. The fishing trip was usually for a fourteen-day period. This hard work was better perhaps than loafing around dockland in a crowded port on the Welsh coast. The trawler skippers knew the Irish coast like the back of their hands, every bay and inlet where they would foray illegally for special fish on moon-lit nights. They knew all the village taverns on the south coast and kept in courteous terms with the proprietors. They loved to take a trip ashore to ease the constant, wearisome routine of a seaman's life. The ultimate aim was to slake a thirst or perhaps in more modern jargon, to have a good 'piss up'. The skippers would bring a full basket of fish as a gift for the tavern landlord, who would reciprocate in suitable fashion. Sometimes an affinity might develop between a salt-seasoned old codger of the deep and the maid behind the bar, who might perchance entice him to return once more, just to admire – even from a distance – a creature so elusive as the landlord's daughter.

Seamen are known to be good-natured and affable creatures, who yearn for female companionship, maybe to break the monotony of the long *trick*. When stepping ashore they become boyish, boisterous and sometimes naughty towards the opposite sex. When free from the confines of ship life, the safety valve of pent up energy is suddenly released, be it in the bright lights of some American port, or the red light district of Marseilles, Mumbai (Bombay) or Hong Kong, where a man's life can be as cheap as a kiss in a brothel. Yet the aura, power and mystery of the sea belong to the sailor alone. This rollicking machismo is a being from another kingdom, a realm far removed from the term 'landlubber', which he will never understand. This is Eros and Cupid of the wave, vagabond lover and ravisher of virginity. Many and various are the ballads relating to his amorous exploits. The sailor seems to be forever saying farewell to his lover, as in this old ballad:

*Fare you well lovely Mollie,*
*I'm now going to leave you,*
*To the western Indies,*
*My course for to steer,*
*Though the big ship be sailing,*
*And the wild waves be raging,*
*I'll come back lovely Mollie,*
*In the spring of the year.*

*I'll dress like a sailor,*
*True love I'll go with you*
*Through the midst of all danger,*
*I'll go without fear,*
*When the big ship is sailing,*
*And the wild waves are raging*
*I'll be with you lovely Johnny,*
*To reef your topsail.*

*Your delicate hands Love,*
*Stout cables cannot handle,*
*And your pretty little feet Love,*
*In the rigging can't go,*
*Your delicate body wild waves can't endure Love,*
*Be advised lovely Mollie to the seas do not go.*

*The big ship set sail,*
*And left Mollie bewailing,*
*Till her cheeks grew pale as the lily that grows.*
*Her gay golden locks,*
*She kept constantly tearing*

*Saying I'll sigh till I die love,*
*Will I e'er see you more?*

Many beautiful sea shanties were sung by sailors in chorus when turning the windlass, for heaving the anchor, raising the great sails or heaving the ropes. For instance, 'The Leaving of Liverpool' and 'The Holy Ground' were known and sung by sailor men the world over.

*The sun is on the harbour love,*
*I cannot now remain,*
*I know it will be*
*Some very long time,*
*Until I see you again,*
*So fare thee well my own true love,*
*When I return united we will be,*
*It's not the leaving of Liverpool,*
*That grieves me,*
*But my darling when I think of thee.*

Before embarking for America on the S.S. *Dresden* of the Hamburg American Line in January 1929, I walked along the famous trysting-place called the Holy Ground. This pathway, which is situated beside the sea, at the eastern brink of Cobh Harbour, was frequented by sailors and their lovers.

*Adieu my lovely Dinah,*
*A thousand times adieu,*
*We must bid goodbye to the Holy Ground,*
*The place that we love true.*
*We will sail the salt seas over*
*And return again for sure,*
*To seek the girls that wait for us,*
*In the Holy Ground once more.*
*Fine girl you are!*
*You're the girl I do adore,*

## A Fisherman Loves His Boat

*And still I live in hope to see,*
*The Holy Ground once more,*
*Fine girl you are!*

The sailing yacht is now the expensive toy of the rich. Modern steamships are oil fuelled or diesel driven, with mod cons for officer and crew alike. Gone are the heady days of the Nelsonian swashbuckling, cutlass wielding, yo, ho and a bottle of rum. Pirate and smuggler, with the Jolly Roger floating gaily from the cross trees, make past history. Despite all, tradition and custom die hard. The sea is still the sailor man's benign or cruel mistress, and ambition for a night ashore his besetting sin. I saw American navy ships pay a courtesy visit to a port on the New England coast. The crew were billed for shore leave on a certain night. It was fascinating to watch bevies of beautiful American girls await the sailors as they stepped ashore. Females of all colours, shapes and size, were perched on every vantage point. It was truly evident the fleet was in. There seemed to be only one Lily of the Lamplight, my own Lily Marlene, waiting at the barrack gate, in contrast with the many lovely girls who have succumbed totally to the advances of this most amorous of creatures, this playboy Casanova of the deep.

## My Boat

*You were no smoking-belching*
*Rusty hulk*
*Looming the horizon,*
*Spilled from the fiery porridge*
*Of a furnace ladle.*

*You were the forest-born one*
*Burst from the womb*
*Of a seed-spilling acorn,*
*A sunglad Spring your midwife*
*Trill of the thrush your birthsong,*
*Reincarnated vibrant planks*
*Alive beneath my feet.*
*My boat,*
*Past memories haunt the furrows*
*Of my mind.*

*Together we grew old.*
*Together we watched pale dawns*
*Replace the dusky canvas*
*Of many a fisher's night.*

*You my faithful ballerina*
*Have danced with me*
*Across the streamfoamed headlands.*
*Together we lie*
*Anchor cast and sail furled,*
*Safe in the harbour of our memories.*

# FISHING FROM THE SHORE

Grey mullet and bass come from the south in the soft tides of early spring, and continue to swim in dense schools into the tidal shallows of our estuaries and warm sandy beaches. The grey mullet is a very oily fish with large scales. It will grow to an average size of four to six pounds. It is a fish that swims very close to the surface; equipped with a gizzard and a sucking mouth, it will revel in following any tidal sea currents containing animal, vegetable or edible oily substances. The fish is much valued for export to the Latin countries.

I watched my father trap the fish in a narrow channel near Ballinskelligs beach, where the school had entered at high water. He laid the net carefully across the channel, mooring it at both ends; he would also stretch a second net three or four yards in front of the first net. The reason for having the second net was that when the mullet found they were trapped, they would jump over the line of the first net, all following each other, like horses over Beecher's Brook, and before they could attain speed enough to jump a second time they became entangled, proving that man's wily ingenuity had bested them. When the tide stranded them we collected about four hundred fine mullet. I remember many were given to neighbours who helped my dad. The rest were sold for a few pence a fish. In those days pence were the euros of today.

Sea bass I do not know so much about, being a full-time fisherman I didn't have enough leisure time to fish on the shore. Bass is a lover of surfy conditions, where heavy rollers breach on the shore, breaking loose minuscule crabs and other organisms from the gravel and sand. It will, on the other hand, frequent quays in a fishing port, coming in on an eddy tide, searching the sea floor for scraps of fish or shrimp which may have fallen from the trawl nets. A ten-pound sea bass is a rugged fish and will fight like a tiger to break you. I know this from my short experience of the ones that got close. We took a fleeting glance at each other and said goodbye.

I was determined to catch at least one sea bass, so rigged myself a strong hemp line, with a four-foot thin steel trace between line and steel pollock hook. Nylon was not heard of until fifty years later. Using some mackerel guts (entrails) for bait, which a bass cannot resist, I was taken by an eight-pound fish on the morning tide; with my crude but effective gear the unfortunate fish didn't have a chance. Roast bass is fine to eat, especially when stuffed with potatoes, breadcrumbs and onions.

I liked line fishing of any kind, bottom fishing in deep water, fishing from rocks in wild isolated cliffs, trolling for pollock. Tempting the unknown with a fishing line held a certain fascination for me, a piece of mackerel on one end and perhaps a damn fool on the other. Fishing for ballan wrasse, when we were boys, on a Sunday, was great fun. It was a pastime my dad did not entirely approve of – 'Keep away from high cliffs', he would say, and how right he was. We could only swim like a stone. Fishing for wrasse from the rocks was dangerous fun. The bait we usually used was lugworm, or crab bait. The sinkers we used were small stones weighing a quarter pound, the bait and hook very close to the sinker. Casting the line into the sea required a certain skill. Many a rock fisherman got a hook stuck in his clothing on making a botched cast, or worse, the hook in the flesh of his hand or finger, such as happened to me. Once was enough. I made sure I never hooked myself again. Then there was the time when Mike Connell pulled up a large red crayfish that got entangled on his line. Mike, who had never seen a crayfish in his life, said it must be the devil complete with horns, beady eyes and claws. He abandoned his line and wouldn't help me to extricate it. I told him it was a crayfish and good to eat. I could not convince him that the red devil was good for anything.

# SHARKS AND OTHER SPECIES

The angler, fishing frog or monkfish, called *anafláig* in the old tongue, has a likeness to a frog because of its great curved semicircular jaws, which are adorned with rows of sharp needle-point teeth on the upper and lower lips. The teeth will grow long in accordance with the size of the fish. The monk is equipped with two great flabby wide cheeks, back of its gills. Sometimes it may not be possible for the fishing frog to consume all it may catch, especially on a day, or perhaps a night, when fishing was good. I often found some uneaten fish stored in the pouches of its great cheeks, for, believe it or not, this ugly disciple of the art is a fish that fishes for a living. Bountiful nature provides the young angler with a new fishing-rod, complete with a pastel grey-blue bait, on its first birthday, and by the time it has attained a length of thirty inches or more, it will be operating three or four fishing-rods. The rods grow from the centre of the backbone in a direct line between head and tail, about six inches apart. They are almost transparent, like nylon, flexible aerials coming to a slender downward loop from which the grey-blue butterfly bait dangles only inches away from the treacherous teeth.

The monkfish can set itself into the sand, or on a rough kelp-grown bottom, with only its eyes exposed and its fishing rods in operation. Only its round stout tail is nowadays much sought after as an expensive fish dish. The creature is not endowed with good looks – in fact it has a most formidable appearance – yet the bountiful Creator did not leave it destitute, equipping it with an ever-lasting supply of free fishing tackle. The fishing frog can be found from the depths of the ocean to the shoals of the harbour.

Many species of shark frequent the South Atlantic coast of Ireland, especially in warm weather conditions. One day while trolling for pollock in a small sixteen-foot punt off Bolus headland, in company with my father, we had occasion to stop while partaking of some lunch. Previously we had disposed of some fresh mackerel entrails over the side. The sea was calm and suddenly we became aware of something solid rubbing against the keel of the boat. My father glanced over the side – he was in the stern seat – and motioned to me to take a look, saying two words only in Irish – *miol draide* – 'grimacing shark', which to me meant only one thing: a man-eating shark. I will describe the shark as best I can. It was a cobalt blue on top, with a great wedge-shaped, blunt nose, and large, round, bright eyes. The underbelly seemed to be a dirty, whitish grey. The most frightening feature was its great semicircular mouth widening beneath its gills like a giant horseshoe, with serrated rows of glistening white saw-teeth adorning what must be its gums, and, as a matter of interest, I noticed some grey marine shell-like growths on its wide back.

Although we were lying in thirty-five fathoms of water, the great fish lay perfectly quiet less than two fathoms beneath our frail craft, frail in comparison to our unwelcome monster visitor whose dorsal fin nearly reached the keel of the punt. As our punt drifted in the current, so too did our visitor with perfect timing. My father said, 'The mackerel guts we threw overboard attracted it.' I said to Dad, 'I'll get the oar and strike the water to scare it off', to which he replied, 'Don't dream of it, we will row towards the headland, near the cliff where we won't have the current to shift us while we're eating.' We put out our oars and rowed gently at slow speed towards Bolus Head. When we reached a place called *Leac an Chinn*, 'the flagstone of the headland', and where the water was still as a duck pond, we shipped our oars once more and proceeded to have our delayed snack in peace. 'He was a big fellow, Dad', I said. 'He was, and a nasty customer to deal with,' replied Dad. 'He had jaws wide enough to swallow a man.'

We had finished our snack and while Dad was fixing his pipe I got the bailer to empty the well under the stern sheeting – we would then resume our pollock fishing. I stood upright in the boat, preparing to get my short paddles into position. Just then I got the shock of a lifetime to see the blunt nose of the ugly shark within inches of our stern. This time I could peer into the gaping circle of its great maw, and look more closely at its glistening rows of sharp band-saw teeth. On the side nearest the boat, the round, bright eye was but mere inches below the water surface. I beckoned to my father, who on surveying the situation, said something like, 'The so-and-so is taking a right look at us this time.' My Dad was by nature very stoic – I could depend on his self-control in the event of a sudden decision. But when Dad asked me to hand him the boat-hook, I thought he had really blown his head gasket. I countered by asking, 'Dad, what in the name of all that is holy do you want the boat-hook for?' Dad replied quietly, 'I'll give it a bang in the eye.' 'Dad, one swish of its great tail will surely swamp us.' Dad answered, 'That is true, but while its tail is well clear of our stern and the body of the punt is in shelter of the Leac, it can't sink us.' I felt little flutterings of some winged creatures in the pit of my food basket. Without any more useless arguments, I handed over the boat-hook. Now, our boat-hook was a solid instrument – it consisted of a nine-foot shaft of ash, with a nine-inch heavy iron spike on top, with a curved hook on one side. This was the time of truth. I can picture my dad standing upright in the stern sheeting and taking careful aim.

I do not know to what warrior, saint or hero I should compare my father, who has departed from life's screen many, many years ago. May he rest in peace. Perhaps he looked like St George and the Dragon, or maybe a Wexford pikeman at Vinegar Hill, or Captain Ahab in pursuit of Moby-Dick. As he thrust the pointed boat-hook with unerring aim at the shark's eyeball, I remember vividly a great curved wide tail lift high in the air behind the boat – the wide wedge-shaped body of the shark exposed for a second – and come crashing down only yards away from our gunwale. Our little punt lurched while salt water rained from the sky in torrents, drenching us to the skin. 'That was a near one, Dad', I ventured. 'It was', Dad retorted, 'but I think that shark must go to see an eye doctor.'

The boat was bailed free of water once again but this time the sea was tossed around like surf on a stormy day. We removed our inside shirts and put on our dry jackets which fortunately we had stored in the bow, it being a warm day in June. There will be some who, no doubt, will be sceptical as to the veracity of my story, but I can honestly assure you I would much rather deal with ghost stories than with rogue sharks. We continued our trolling for pollock undisturbed for the rest of the evening.

On another occasion I heard my father tell how old Patrick Barry of Horse Island, together with a helper fisherman and a little boy, were chased by a thresher or killer shark which kept continually leaping out of the water within feet of their rowing boat. They were shipping water disturbed by the shark's continual broaching. It was only when they collected some foul-smelling bilge water that was lodged in the bottom of the boat, and fed it into the wake of the boat, did the shark desist from worrying them. Sharks do not like foul-smelling water.

Another immense inhabitant of the deep is the great basking shark, which can be found in our south and west inshore waters in early spring and summer. Among the many names in Irish for the basking shark, one finds *iamlhán gréine, ainmhí na seolta, cearbhán, seoltóir* and *liopadaileap*. The authorities differ on the exact location of their breeding ground, somewhere in the depths of the South Atlantic. All the information I have gathered from observation of their annual movement is that they seem to approach the Irish coast from the south-west and swim north, entering the shallow bays and estuaries.

I had experience of one basking shark that became entangled in a fishing net. We had to tow it ashore to recover some part of our gear, which turned out a total loss. It was a creature of huge dimensions. It measured thirty-seven feet in length and seventeen feet in girth. I remember having taken pains to measure it accurately. The basking shark is not a dangerous shark – in fact its gullet is very narrow and is equipped with a series of vertical plates on each side that act as filters through which plankton is strained. Fishmeal manufacturers have bought the huge carcasses of red beef-like meat. The shark is most prized for its huge liver. One liver produces seventeen casks of oil when rendered. The sharks usually swim in pairs close to the surface at very slow speed, following the warm sea currents, some of which have a rich mixture of several species of plankton. This shark is not aggressive and does not pose a threat to fisher folk or swimmers.

There exist many leviathan denizens of the deep oceans that have never been exposed to the gaze of man. Hundreds of different species of shark live in the tropics, also many hundred species of turtle, and in some Australian and Oriental waters live large and poisonous sea snakes.

Very few fishermen ever get close enough to the round leather-tan grampus to get a detailed picture of this enormous sea monster which some call 'the herring hog'. Only on two occasions in my life have I witnessed it broaching the surface, and then only exposing a long looping coil rolling downwards into the depths, a brown leathery gloss on its skin and not showing any fins. All I could say – its body was round like an earthworm and of immense girth. It must have weighed tons judging from the amount of water it displaced when it surfaced.

The blue porbeagle shark, which in Irish is called *an preabaire gorm*, is much sought after by rod and reel sportsmen. It requires very high-breaking strain lines, powerful reels and heavy fibreglass rods to bring a porbeagle to the gaff. Shark-fin soup is supposedly supped in chic eating-houses and as I have never tasted the delicacy, I must not be critical in matters of appetizing taste.

The common dogfish, or *madra glas*, spike dogfish, is a near cousin of the shark family and as a fisherman it did not help me commercially, domestically or otherwise to become involved with spur dogs. Only one time, when fish became very scarce in the last World War, was there a demand for flake dogfish. Then, the export price did not justify the labour in skinning, icing and boxing.

I remember a night when a train of herring nets got badly torn by a school of spur dog. Not content in gorging with live herring, they can tear an expensive net to tatters while doing so. Spike dogfish are a voracious species. I have seen them drag little guillemot chicks beneath the water and devour them. The spur female can give birth to six fully developed pups, complete with spikes and fins, all ready to do for themselves, each with a transparent sac attached to its navel containing a yellow yolk exactly comparable to that of a hen egg. In this sac, I have been informed, nature has provided enough vitamins via an umbilical cord to its stomach, until the young dog is able to fend for itself.

Dog fish are equipped with two sharp spikes near the back and dorsal fins. I have special reason to remember a day when a dog spike was driven deep into the flesh near my shinbone. I remember my father washed out the wound with seawater, and encouraged the puncture to bleed more by enlarging the entrance to the cut with the point of a small penknife. After several more washings in the brine, although it was painful and stiff, it cured from the word go. My dad was a great believer in plenty of air and sunlight for wounds. Being only a *garsún* of twelve tender years, and unable to control the muscular swishing tail of a twelve-pound spur dog, the encounter I speak of only served to infuse in me a healthy respect for the species that lasted the duration of my career as a fisherman.

*An chaillleach bhreac*, the grey hag, and the great spotted dogfish are related in blood and bone, except for one redeeming feature – the grey hag does not have the formidable spike. The grey hag has a serpent-like appearance, is an ugly-looking fish and not commercially profitable in the fish food chain; inshore waters can become totally infested with it and become a nightmare for trammel-net fishermen when there is one in every mesh.

The female hag will lay an elongated, opaque, cigar-shaped purse some months after copulation; attached to the purse are four sensitive tendrils which twine and curl around the kelp stems, anchoring them until the purse will open and young dogfish will emerge, with a yolk for sustenance. I do not know how many purse eggs are laid by one female. Skate and ray also lay large flat purses in the shape of the letter H.

Some fishermen call another large-type species 'the white hound'. The old Irish name was *fámaire*, meaning of course 'the robust, overgrown, muscular fellow'. This species is called a tope. It is more shark than dogfish. I happened to take one some years ago, when sea angling. I had quite a struggle to get it into the small boat. It kept rolling over and over and weighed in excess of sixty pounds. The maw and open jaws are like the blue shark, except that the tope is a greyish white. They are also voracious eaters. In one tope's stomach I found three large mackerel, one large black sole and one medium pollock. Why I performed this gory, gutty operation was to retrieve my steel hook, trace and swivel the white hound had swallowed into the nethermost region of its stomach. It is also interesting to note that each mackerel had its tail severed, as if by a sharp knife, thus the name *gearrthóir*, 'cutter'.

Having nothing more interesting to occupy my time in the Depression of the early thirties in the great USA – in which country I was allowed to stay under a valid immigration quota – I sat on the end of a wooden pier at a place called Savin Rock, outside New Haven, on the shore of Long Island Sound. With some sand lugs for bait, I often got some flounders and blue fish when they were running. But not tonight. Poor Irish Yorik immigrant, I could only land one solitary wriggling sandpaper-skin, eye-blinking son of a spotted dogfish, *cailleach bhreac*, which must have chased the liner all the way from Skelligs Rock to the tip of Sandyhook. I rubbed my eyes to examine my contorting catch more closely – yes, there was no difference between the Old Hag of Béara and the grey hag of Long Island Sound.

Dolphins and porpoise are seen to congregate in great schools as they approach the coast at the end of May. Some fisher folk regard this as a prediction of a fine summer to come. The porpoise will hunt the early salmon schools, and also the sturgeon. They can pursue their quarry for days without end, until finally encircling and closing in for the kill. Porpoise and dolphins are not dangerous to swimmers, are highly intelligent creatures, and have shown a certain curious affinity towards humans. Sometimes they stray from their herd when they come into shallow waters and can be trapped. The natives of the Polynesian Islands in the far Pacific had a chant, which they called 'porpoise calling'. They would stand on the reefs when the wind was favourable to carrying the sound of their voices far offshore. In perhaps a matter of days the porpoise schools would follow the music of the chant into a narrow channel where they were harvested for their meat, liver and skins.

# SQUID, CUTTLEFISH AND OCTOPUS

Squid, cuttlefish and octopus can be found in almost all seas of the world. The lobsterman is well-acquainted with the octopus, who will avail of a free meal from the lobster pot whenever possible. Thankfully, the octopus will not grow to a large size in North Atlantic waters and does not pose a threat to swimmers or divers. Only in warm tropical waters are they known to endanger life. We know it by names such as 'the devil's hook' – *crúcaí an diabhail.* Even a small one with eight tentacles, ten inches long, equipped with hundreds of razor-sharp cutting discs, can become an ugly customer to deal with. Drastic measures have to be used to make it relax its tentacles. It can change the colour of its skin to suit that of its surroundings. It has two evil-looking, small, blue-green eyes, and is capable of changing shape as well as colour.

All squid are equipped with an ink sac which they use to squirt into the face of an attacking adversary. The torpedo-shaped squid, with side vanes, is a milky grey opaque colour, with soft streamer tentacles, without the disc teeth of its cousin, the octopus, and is used as a speciality in the table menu of many restaurants. In Mediterranean countries the octopus is used widely for its food value. It is processed, cured, sometimes dried in the intense heat of the sun. Octopus soup can be very palatable.

The only bone in the squid is its backbone structure, which is not bone as is common to other marine species. The back of the squid is a structure of brittle white gritty lime-like substance, very lightweight, and will float buoyantly on water. It is oval-shaped, and in early spring it can be found washed ashore on beaches of the world. The pre-Christian Irish called it the *teanga bó bailbhe,* 'dumb cow's tongue', connecting it to the mythology of the Fianna, and 'the Land of Youth', *Tír na nÓg*. The 'dumb cow's tongue' is sold commercially to aviaries and bird-fanciers, as an important form of mineral grit for the life of all cage birds.

Another squid is the deep water cuttlefish with a beak-like bottlenose; this species can grow several metres long and is not known to frequent shallow water. I have often witnessed large schools of cuttlefish come to the surface, leaping and cavorting. They will also take artificial bait, like red rubber, or feather.

# SPAWN

Female fish spawn eggs and roe, while milt is the spawn of male fish. The egg and the milt must meet so that all different order of life will continue to survive on earth. The pale pink herring roe, which is so nice to eat, has a million eggs packed tightly in a separate space within the flexible tissue of two cigar-like membranes, joined by a slender cord of tissue near the centre. The milt of the male herring is a grey-white fatty substance, and is also edible – nice when fried to a crisp.

I heard the name *eochair*, Irish for roe, and the name *leadhbhán*, Irish for milt, used by my parents. I do not know of any other form of Irish name except *sceith* used by the neighbours. *Sceith* means spawn, both roe and milt.

The harvest herrings were full to the gills with rich roe – only the red gills were removed when being prepared for curing. When washed and packed, lying on their backs, in wooden 150-lb casks, the salt herring and mackerel were sold on local markets and sometimes exported. The Germans made roll fillets, held together by a little wooden peg. They were preserved in jars and sold as pickled herring, to be eaten raw.

Herring roe is much sought after at the moment by the Japanese; it is processed to become an expensive caviar. The roe of the whiting is a pink flesh-colour. When browned and roasted it becomes brittle and delicious to eat. The male whiting's milt is thin and watery and is not used as food.

In springtime the codfish is heavy with roe. According to the size of the fish, the roe stocking can weigh several pounds, containing millions of small eggs like round beads in dense formation. It is sold in fish markets by weight and is more expensive than the same portion of codfish. The male milt of the cod has less commercial value. All species of fish have different roe pods, some having a flavour delicious to taste, but all are nourishing to the human body, full of vitamins, minerals, phosphorus, iron, etc., etc.

White pollock, glossan pollock, also called 'Black Jacks', or in Irish *gréasaí*, and other large fish (for example, ling) are seen to congregate in special spawning beds, free from swift underwater currents, in waters as shallow as 30 fathoms.

The spawning ground is usually what is termed 'speckled ground' – *talamh breac* in Irish. The *talamh breac* would present to the readers an undersea garden, with acres of floor space, complete with rock pools, gravel beds, sandy valleys, kelp and sea grass, in fields sheltered by ridges of rock, high beds of stripe and rod kelp. The rough fish I have described have come back from the depths of the ocean since time immemorial to these marine gardens , from January to the middle of February, in order to deposit their seed in their birthplace. I do not know how it all started, and at the risk of being scoffed at, all I can say, with the Psalmist, is:

*O Lord, I love the beauty of thy house*
*and the place where thy glory dwelleth.*

The roe of mackerel is a reddish pink colour, the eggs and the pod much smaller. It has an oily flavour like that of the mackerel itself. The horse mackerel roe is also very rich in fatty oil. In olden times the oil of its liver was melted down to provide rush wick light in primitive, shell oil lamps.

A rare fish in inshore waters is the *scadán capaill*, or 'shad'. I only found shad herring a few times, never in any quantity. Shad roe is much sought after in the United States and is a very expensive food item. I have watched fishermen trolling for shad on Long Island Sound, USA.

Gurnard roe is rich in savoury protein and will make a soup which is nectar to the buds of the palate.

All shellfish have roe, and spawn. The female lobster, called a *faoisceán* in Irish, when full of spawn is called a 'berry hen' because the spawn when ripe resembles a cluster of blackberries. The spawn is attached to the undercarriage sections of the lobster's broad tail. The eggs are a glossy blue, like turnip seed, but get larger and pink at the time of being shed and are very tasty if eaten raw. It is illegal for a fisherman to take or market a berry hen.

Crayfish eggs are similar to lobsters', except red in colour. The large red edible crab develops the spawn underneath the centre opening shield after being first fertilized by the male species, as is also the case with crayfish and lobsters. The male lobster and crab are referred to in Irish as *collach*, meaning 'a boar'. The spawn of the crab is very sponge-like, the millions of very small eggs bound together in dark brown hair-like tissue. All the various species of crab have a similar pattern of spawn. While the eggs ripen, the underneath shield is forced outward and will not close until the entire spawn is shed. The same spawn pattern relates to the shrimp and prawn family. The mollusc and bivalves all contain eggs and roe. Some, like the escallop, are delicious to eat.

I never found roe in conger eels, and I do not have any knowledge of their spawning cycle. The white whelk spawn, which in Irish is called *faochóg chapaill*, or 'horse winkle', deposit their eggs in such a way that they cling to each other, forming spongy balls with separate cells like bee's honeycomb. They are to be found between underwater reefs, where short kelp and carrageen moss abound in tidal reefs near the shoreline. I never found ripe roe in ballan wrasse. The roe develop in the winter months when the fish seem to seek the deep water because the inshore rocks have shed the mussels on which they feed.

# OBSERVATIONS OF A FISH-GUTTER

During my life as a fisherman, I have removed the entrails from many tons of fish. This process is called gutting. Why did I do this gutting? Preparing the fish for market or for curing, of course.

Over the passing years, I haven't been able to help noticing the many strange similarities in nature. My most important implement used in the profession of gutting fish has been a whetted steel knife with a seven-inch razor-sharp blade. An old saying: a dull blade is a waste of time, and another saying: a fisherman without his knife or a wagon without a wheel.

What did I find during my many years of apprenticeship in gutting? The word dissecting I will leave to my more professional friends, who deal with frogs and white mice. I found that fish have bodies with skin, some with more layers than others. They have heads, with eyes, some that blink, eyes large and beautifully coloured, others formidable and evil-looking, slanting and bead-like eyes. Some pelagic fish take on a thick film-like growth covering part of the pupil of the eye in late autumn, which will disappear again in spring. Mackerel is one such fish.

Some fish have attractive features, coloured eyebrows; some have fat upper lips and rows of enamel white teeth, like the ballan wrasse, which will feed on the young mussel growth. Others have needle teeth, like hake, and some saw-tipped and in double rows. The conger has powerful jaw muscles but small teeth. All fish have a nose of some kind. Some have beaks with the usual orifices. Many fish – haddock, cod, red gurnard etc. – wear whiskers in the form of little tails under the chin.

Now for the clothes they wear – the fish scales, little plates of tough plastic-like film arranged in perfect watertight sequence like roof tiles. This thermal clothing provided by nature is a beautiful multicoloured raiment, which adorns the cuckoo wrasse, red bream, Atlantic salmon and dragonet.

Some fish brains I have found very pleasing to the palate – salmon brain and ballan wrasse are extremely succulent. The brain is contained in a case, or compartment, of opaque gristle, in the skull structure, usually between the eyes. Some have left and right divisions. The lungs are protected by the gill plates: a series of blood-filled minute tender fronds. These are the breathing organs that extract oxygen from the water. Fish have air sacs, some with double pressure bladders like red block nose gurnard, which can resist deep-water pressures.

The palate and tongue of cod make a savoury soup. Do fish have taste buds? Perhaps they do! I know some fish like special bait. Fish can communicate by sound or some form of underwater sonar or fish talk. Gurnard when taken on board make distinct croaking frog sounds. Conger can cough like a human. Red bream make a thin whining sound; crayfish make corncrake sounds by rubbing two base plates of its antenna poles together. Of course fish have throats and tongues and perhaps can sing and make merry – at least they have plenty to drink.

Fish have a navel and an anus, with a centre plexus of nerve fibres situated near the outer circle of the anus, on the underbelly. The old Gaelic fisher folk called this area *na deilgneacha*, meaning the thorns. A smart blow using a wooden baton or blunt instrument delivered by the fisherman on the plexus of thorns was enough to paralyse the more unruly species of fish, including dogfish, tope or blue shark.

Fins are the limbs by which fish propel themselves, with dorsal, pectoral underbelly stabilizing fins. The entire section from the tail to the dorsal fin moves in a fast side to side movement, making the fish move forward – in which direction is controlled by the nerve signals of the fish brain.

Fish have very nice blood-red, oval-shaped hearts, complete (I assume) with all the auricles, valves and ventricles that constitute the mechanics of a good pump. What are the functions of the heart pump? – to pump blood through a complicated network of channels called veins and arteries, which I have found in fish. I am told that fish are cold-blooded creatures. Now I ask myself the question – how cold is cold blood? How hot is hot blood? And what is the temperature of living fish blood? During my fish-gutting, most servile, occupation, I have found that vapour arises from the bloody guts of a freshly caught fish. Will some marine biologist out there please rescue me from the abyss of my rustic ignorance before I snuff it – what is the blood temperature of living, swimming, pelagic fish?

A few fish, such as grey mullet and others, have gizzards perhaps to grind shell. In my curiosity, while gutting, I have discovered that the gizzard contains particles of coarse stone and tiny white grit. I have no doubt that fish, like other, land-based, animals, are prone and vulnerable to disease. Some fish are naturally thin and spent after spawning, such as herring, mackerel, cod, haddock, etc. – this is all a natural cycle. The fish quickly recover and start to put on a healthy colour and appearance once more.

Many fish I have found emaciated and lean beyond description. To my amazement I found hard growths, some dark greenish dry lumps that crumbled easily between my fingers, blockages within the stomach and the entrails. I found this when such fish should be in the peak of condition. In my old age I suspect that fish die from some ailment akin to cancer. Fish, after spawning – especially all edible fish that I have gutted – had stomachs, intestines, livers, gall bladders, filled with green, acid-tasting fluid, which the fisherman is careful not to burst when removing, to avoid tainting of the fish for cooking.

Both male and female fish have reproductive organs, roe sacs in the female for thousands of eggs, milt sacs in the male to produce liquid sperm. The skeleton structure of pelagic and demersal species consists of a spinal backbone, complete with spools, discs, breast cage ribs, spinal sac and cord. Some back spools contain a succulent juice which when chewed I suspect is a kind of fish marrow.

Turbot can bleed profusely if a vein near the base of the spine is severed. This will make the fish more palatable. The nerve system of a conger eel will remain active for a long period after it is presumed dead. Several species of pelagic fish can become infested with a marine kind of flesh worm. The parasite is worm-like, coiled in a circular form, usually living in the fish wall of the belly. Cod, wrasse, pollock, haddock, when in thin condition, especially after spawning, are subject to an infestation of this kind; or fish caught on a barren seabed, usually called by fishermen 'hungry ground'.

I have skinned several species of fish and cured the skin of sole, red bream and others, with a solution of alum salt and oak bark – the process used in tanning leather successfully.

To conclude, a fisherman's job is not limited to that of catching large quantities of fish which admittedly, is the main aim of his intended plan. Manifold and various are the other parts he must be able to turn his hand to, 'ere he can call it a day. I do not wish to list the many tasks, too numerous to mention, for God knows the good trawler man was often called upon to be chief cook, bottle washer, mate, deck-hand and fish-gutter combined.

# THE GULF STREAM

Why should I write about the Gulf Stream? What knowledge do I have regarding that great current of warm water which flows northwards from the Gulf of Mexico, up by the eastern coast of the United States, bringing us billions of tons of heated water, to mix with the cold icy waters of the North Atlantic in an area called the Grand Banks of Newfoundland, covering several hundred square miles. Renowned for its abundance of cod and halibut, where a steaming pea-soup fog is always experienced by mariners. It will swirl to a height of hundreds of feet, blotting out all visibility, while a stiff breeze on the surface of the sea will not reduce the steaming condensation.

One arm of the great warm flood penetrates north-west until it reaches the coast of Canada; the other arm runs directly across the

Atlantic to the south-west coast of Ireland to part once more at Skellig Michael, where one branch turns north along the west coast and the other to the south. I have found coconuts from time to time, some at sea for long periods judging by the several coatings of long-stemmed barnacles; the fruit was yet edible.

The many marine species of jellyfish – some huge, globular, umbrella-shaped creatures, with long trailing tentacles equipped with stings; others resemble open parachutes, such as the 'Portuguese man-of-war', which has a series of multicoloured fringes. Others have orange-coloured fringes continually opening and closing as a means of propulsion. Another blue jellyfish that is shaped like a boat is called 'Before the wind sailor'. It comes all the way up from the Bermudas. The little boat is usually not more than three inches in length, always submerged except for a blunt blue pyramid-like sail showing about an inch above the surface. The colour is a cobalt blue. Many of the hundred different coelenterate species described by marine biologists as jellyfish can sting, raise skin rash and blisters and can be very poisonous. Bathers are advised to avoid contact with them. The Gaels of Ireland, Scotland and the Isle of Man refer to the jellyfish as *smugairle róin*, 'a snotty spit from a seal'!

The flood of warm water is a life-enriching injection to all marine creatures that live and grow in our coastal seas, helping to propagate the dense growth of plankton and other organisms vital for the sustenance of fish and bird life.

I have seen the green leatherback turtle near Bolus headland in Ballinskelligs. This species is not edible. The creature will grow to an immense size, perhaps as much as half a ton weight. Its breeding ground is deep within the Gulf of Mexico. Marine biologists tell us the turtle will swim north for long distances and have recorded them close to the Arctic Circle. However, they admit they have not solved the full story of the green turtle's migratory cycle as of yet. It is one of the only species that feed on jellyfish, and a warning has been issued to shipping not to dump small plastic bags while at sea. The green leatherback will swallow the plastic containers, mistaking them for a jellyfish, resulting in the death of numerous turtles whose digestive organs become obstructed and fail to function.

A deceased friend of mine, Walter Scott Green, who was sailing home to California after a trip to Europe, had intended to visit Ireland, where he had parental roots – unfortunately, certain circumstances didn't allow him to fulfil his wish. It was his disappointment prompted him to ask one of the stewards of the S.S. *Marsdam* to provide him with three empty bottles at a point two hundred miles south-west of Ireland. Into each bottle he put his name and address and a copy of the Gospel of St John in three languages. Going on deck the night of 15th October 1967, with a little prayer he consigned the bottles to the waves, hoping someone in Ireland might by chance find his prayer message and send him a reply.

Some six days after, two of his bottles were found at beaches in Ballinskelligs Bay, about two miles apart. Some weeks later the third bottle drifted ashore near a fishing village in the Quebec area, Canada. This is proof positive regarding the direction and power of the Gulf Stream. On finding the bottle and his message, I hastened to reply immediately by airmail to his address at Laguna Beach, California. How surprised he was to find my letter awaiting him when he arrived home. The reason was, Walter had disembarked from the S.S. *Marsdam* at Boston, and had travelled overland to California. But 'bottle post', plus the Gulf Stream, had beaten him to it.

Walter and his wife remained steadfast friends of mine until he – a man who believed in goodness – was called to his reward. That is another story. May he rest in peace.

This warm flood that gives us a temperate climate also has many other diverse ways of affecting our weather pattern. Down there in the deep womb of the Gulf, the seeds of great equinoctial hurricanes are produced, swirling, spiralling, speeding and spreading like giant rotating discs across the southern waters of the North Atlantic, gathering wind speeds of more than one hundred miles per hour, causing havoc to shipping and coastal areas, dumping inches of rain on Ireland, until they spend their destructive force in the vastness of the North Atlantic. South-westerly winds are the most prevailing for the Kerry coast, giving the green isle its name.

Tropical plants will grow profusely in the Iveragh Peninsula – eucalyptus, fuchsia, even the Californian redwood will survive. Arum lilies will grow outdoors – all giving evidence of the warmth.

Schools of triggerfish, which were rarely seen some years ago, are becoming commonplace. The clinging warm misty banks of white sea fog which envelop our south coast in spring and early summer give the impression that the great Reeks of the Kerry mountains are forever shrouded in cotton wool. This is only part of the gentle legacy left to Ireland by the bountiful Gulf Stream.

*I will go down to the sea today,*
*Down to the harbour strand,*
*Where I can smell the frothy spume,*
*The kelp and the wet sea sand.*
*Where white sails are gently filling*
*Gliding like wraiths through the mist*
*In a fisherman's heart is a singing*
*The bountiful wind from the west.*

# BLACK GOLD, BLACK HOLES

Once upon a time, we heard of gold strikes and other elements that, when harnessed, were for the benefit of mankind. Now we have black gold spilled into the oceans and washed onto our shores, leaving our beaches polluted with vast clots of thick, viscous oil. I have found many species of seabirds, even dolphins and seals, blinded by oil, many suffering horrible death. Wars have been fought, lives have been lost, millions have been squandered, to prove who should have the final control over sale and commercial distribution of black gold.

An academic friend of mine posed a question: As a layperson what do you think of the present age of new technology? The only answer I can give: I'm glad to have witnessed this change; for me it is an exciting time to be alive. I approve of wonderful new dwellings, all the modern appliances, air travel, communications, etc., etc. I love to see two animated blobs of clay out there in space, cleaning the Hubble telescope, anchored to their mother shuttle by their most unnatural umbilical cords. I love to hear parents complaining how best we control TV, video and the Internet, etc., because blue porn is available to their darling offspring. Don't get me wrong – I'm not a spoilsport. I love to hear religious mystics together with scientists debate the age of the universe, telling the viewing audience they make the assumption the 'Big' something 'Bang' banged fifteen thousand million years ago, and I stand accused by own dear ones of having suffered a lapse of memory once in a century. The religious mystics play around with the spiritual entity that survives the body after death; beyond that, they stop short of making me feel happy, by telling me about a life hereafter or the joys of Paradise.

'Poltergeists' are taboo. Scientists describe this phenomenon as controlled energy. Others say it is a spirit not resting in peace. But so long as the furniture is not thrown around and doors stay on their hinges, mum's the word. I do not mind if it only happens in your house – the professor shrugs his shoulders, and murmurs, 'All old hat.'

They keep on educating poor Yorik, layman, on cause and effect, chaos and order, black holes, novas, plus supernovas, pulsars, light years, new stars being born, old ones dying, another sceptical TV programme on Star Wars, one for the archives, and finally, for the wheelie bin. Then I ask myself, why should I be doubting Thomas? Why should I be a crank, because I see whole stretches of rivers completely wiped out? Fish kills are the order of the day. Our streams, rivers and lakes are becoming sewers. Thanks to uncontrolled use of fertilizer and farm effluent, our lakes lack oxygen, not possessing enough to sustain a healthy fishing life. The result: algae growth and decay.

Time was, when we blamed the poacher. Are we so blinded now that we do not recognize the real culprit?

## OLD WEATHER SIGNS AND SUPERSTITIONS

The moon and its phases were part and parcel of Irish country life and inescapably linked with folklore in what could now be termed our superstitious past. This thinking changed overnight since modern man set foot on its surface. The roller-blind of mystery has lifted and suddenly laid bare the myth and the wonder which inspired great enthusiasm in peoples of every class and creed. Alas, the sheen of moonlight has lost some of its special qualities, the inspiration of poets and lovelorn unhappiness – 'The Moon behind the Hill'. How disappointed I was to hear that the moon was a vast and lonely place, rock-strewn and dusty – only a mirror held in the invisible hand of gravity, reflecting the light of a giant atomic furnace back to our spinning blue top, lighting a bedtime candle for us children born of darkness. Yet all seems in perfect balance. Now that we have partly satisfied our curiosity, how has it changed our thinking? Applying the question to myself, I feel my belief a little dented, for my roots go back to pre-Christian Ireland, when my ancestors were good, law-abiding druids who worshipped fire and water. We had our own shamans, leeches and astrologers long before a meteorological service was set up in Ireland. The time was when *Mugh Roith*, Arch Druid of Ireland, had a summerhouse in *Oileán Dairbhre*, Valentia Island, Uíbh Ráthach, Co. Kerry, and another in *Cnoc Loinge*, Knocklong in Co. Limerick. No doubt he enjoyed island life, even if he didn't have a whirligig.

Some of *Mugh Roith's* old weather signs must have rubbed off on us, such as *súil choiligh*, meaning 'a cock's eye', showing the moon encircled by a golden ring, the same golden ring as referred to in that impressive poem 'Wreck of the Hesperus', a veritable precursor of storm. A wide halo of light, often seen around the sun, a telltale sign of rain. Old fishermen would watch for a break in the halo – this they called *béal na gaoithe*, or 'mouth of the wind', and it revealed the direction from which the wind and rain would follow. I heard expressions in Irish like: *Tá an ré ag féachaint breoite anocht*, 'The moon looks sickly tonight.' A brilliant shining moon in a clear cloudless sky is a sign of settled weather.

The Native Americans had much the same superstition as the Irish in relation to the moon. If the crescent new moon lay on its back, the Indians expected dry weather, believing it held water in its hollow cup. If it stood erect in the sky it spilled the water out. The direct opposite was the Irish superstition. The magnetic influence of the moon in its phases was noticed by country folk to play a part in the natural routine of their lives. They observed that the moon controlled the rise and fall of tides with exact perpetual precision. People who suffered from mental illness were found to be more stable when the moon was on the wane. Osiers and twigs grown for basket making were less elastic for twisting and weaving if cut in the full of the moon.

Shellfish, especially edible red crab, were found to be more palatable in the dark moon. Fishermen said the meat had less water content. The rising moon showing a red rusty colour in summer prophesied warm weather. Sailors were very concerned if a planet was seen in line with the moon, an omen of stormy conditions. Dogs howl pitifully, and the primitive dogs – the wolf, coyote, etc. – all sing their mating call during full moon. Other animals – birds, bats, owls, corncrakes, willow-warblers, hedgehogs, badgers, foxes, rabbits and hares, and those not entirely nocturnal – all enjoy and revel in the light of the moon.

White castle clouds rising majestically in an azure blue sky signified cold showers to come, sometimes accompanied with hail, and spectacular rainbows. Cumulus clouds rising like giants, nodding their ugly heads behind one another, with a more horrible grotesque back-cap cloud pumping up suddenly in the background, as if demanding a grandstand view – *Ag bagairt a gcinn thar dhroim a chéile* – as appears in the epic 'Midnight Court' by

Merriman. Turbulence and agitation among the clouds aloft told of an approaching thunderstorm. Small white puffball clouds scudding before a dark background betokened wind and rain soon to follow.

> *If the wind comes before the rain*
> *You shall soon set sail again.*
> *If the rain comes before the wind*
> *Tie down your sails and to the anchor swing.*

One of the most unwelcome signs was pothooks on the horizon. I only witnessed the phenomenon once while fishing off the Skelligs. It was evening time, with a light southerly breeze and a gentle heaving sea. Conditions ideal for trawling and fishing excellent – in fact all the best fish were on the wave. A trawl full of prime fish was the reward for a three-hour drag. Suddenly after sundown, a spectacular array of pothooks started to appear on the line which divides sky and ocean, looming larger and more menacingly as night approached. The wind and sea increased with steady combined momentum, finally forcing us to stow our gear and run for shelter. During the night a violent storm developed with an accompanying heavy sea. That evening confirmed for me that pot-hooks on the horizon were not to be taken lightly and that a fisherman must at all times be alert, keeping the weather eye open.

White 'mares' tails' extending from north-east to west, in a high sky with green-blue pastel background, promised dry windy days from a north-easterly direction. Sheep's fleece, *bearradh caorach,* showed change for rain after a dry spell. Mackerel-skin pattern in south-east sky, wind and prolonged rain to follow. 'Red sky on high, sunshine is nigh' – *dearg ard grian amáireach.* Blackbirds whistling in the dawn told of rain and mist for the coming day – *feadáil lon ar maidin ceo 'gus fearthainn.* 'A rainbow in the morning is the shepherd's warning; a rainbow at night is the shepherd's delight.' Rainbows at night are a rare occurrence and are only seen when conditions are favourable, with bright moonlight shining through soft misty showers, producing sometimes a double arc of rainbow in a translucent light – in past days seen as a happy augur that fine weather would ensue. White clouds like sea-urchins, or giants with thorn bush beards, portended cold wintry showers of hailstone. 'Sun legs' in the morning for wind, 'sun legs' in the evening for calm – this is how my parents foretold the weather in their own simple way – *cosa gaoithe ar maidin, cosa cailm tráthnóna*. White fog on a marsh at dawn – a sign of rain. Cotton-wool fog on mountain peaks – a sign of settled weather to come.

Short rainbow stubs at both sides of the setting sun were called foxtails – in Irish *madra,* meaning 'a dog'. These are the reflection of the sun's rays on an approaching depression. Country folk did not welcome the dog. The foxtail when visible at the south of the sinking sun informed us that the depression was moving southward. A copper-coloured bright glare in the sky over the orb of the setting sun denoted cold windy wet weather to come.

I learned from listening to my parents and to the kind neighbours who came to our house to pass the long winter nights in harmless conversation, always in the unadulterated Irish tongue, which in my case was an added advantage, as English was not my best way of expression at the time. My neighbour's house, 'Siobhán's', was but a pebble-throw apart, just across the field. Siobhán was very old, finishing the last few years of a century. Her house was a special all-Irish club where elderly men, some unmarried, would gather to smoke their pipes and talk. Wet nights were a godsend. In the old thatched cabin a single-burner paraffin oil lamp and blazing peat fire cast a flickering warm light on lime washed walls. The southerly wind, loaded with thick raindrops beating an incessant tattoo on the glass drums of the small windows, helped us appreciate the cosy interior of the kitchen. Surely, a stage-set night for storytelling. Jamesie Taig was a good storyteller who would put flesh on the bones of the most incredible tale. He believed in pookas, banshees, premonitions, and would swear by the holy light all to be true. At times, overwhelmed by his own imaginative exuberance, he would break the barrier of reasonable exaggeration, but when spoken in the pure Munster of his mother tongue – used with power and authority – I could forgive him for making pookas loom as large as Skelligs Rock.

Then there was Tomaseen Sugrue, raconteur par excellence, telling tales of historical importance relating to the flamboyant lifestyle of some local landlords, in which he showed an inbuilt abhorrence regarding their social behaviour. If I had only wisdom enough then to understand I was getting free education, *ach is fada dhó ráite nach féidir cloigeann críon a chur ar cholainn óg*, 'the impossibility of putting an old head on young shoulders'. Tomaseen held the belief that the sea was entirely feminine – grammatically correct from a language point of view – from the many rich folktales he had heard handed down from knee to knee, and from sire to son. The sea he described was a female spirit which becomes fertile once in a given period of time, and brims over and will surprise us, because we do not know the whole story of how the earth has life to renew and continue.

All animals – birds, fish and insects – are endowed with a pre-awareness of changing weather patterns. Birds have been known to behave strangely, even to move their young to higher ground before great storms. Schools of salmon approaching the coast will display a lively exhilaration by leaping wildly and erratically on the surface at the approach of an oncoming rainstorm. It was at Siobhán's academy that I first became indoctrinated in the language of the strands or the beaches. Weather signs were not confined to what the eye observed during daylight. At night the trained ear of coast dwellers and old fishermen came into play as well.

Tomaseen, on arriving at Siobhán's to take his seat among the neighbours, would declare to all and sundry, '*Cloisim Tráigh an Bhearna Dhearg ag labhairt anocht. Tá gaoth ón raithnigh chugainn*', which meant he could hear the surf breaking on the Beach of the Red Gap that foretold wind from the hills where the ferns (*raithneach*) grow. In later years I became accustomed to the language of strands, the sound of the waves crashing on the beach, reverberating through the night air, obliterating other sounds of nature. I would hear my father say, '*Tá Trá Bhuaile Chaoil ag bagairt gaoth aneas.*' – 'Boolakeel Strand is threatening us with southerly wind.'

Each strand had its own special sound which when decoded by the local aborigines gave us a correct weather forecast, proving our early warning system was functioning perfectly.

Keel Strand in St Finan's Bay was a broadcaster of stormy conditions, especially if the soughing sound of the waves carried in the air currents over the hill into Ballinskelligs. The sound in this case seemed to come from the sky. The old folk would say, 'Keel Strand is speaking broken weather.' – '*Tá Trá na Cille ag labhairt aimsir bhriste chug-ainn.*' Many other sea sounds, and wave patterns, such as 'cats paws' (small jumping little hillocks, which denote sudden wind changes), and boiling, bubbling, broken water (forerunner of a sudden drop in wind pressure) – all these signs had meaningful connotations for fisherman and farmer alike.

The awesome booming of the breaking billows teaching us the now primitive language of the strands and beaches I first heard of in Siobhán's rambling house, today are part of the mellowing, shrinking cells of my brain.

A little blue window appearing in an overcast sky was a sign of a clearance soon to come, known to seafaring men as 'a Dutchman's trousers'. Frogs and snails seen in numbers near farmyards gave warning of damp, humid conditions to prevail; likewise, our own open-breasted chimney served as an accurate barometer. After a reasonable dry spell, little balls of black soot would suddenly become dislodged form the interior of the chimney breast, to come bouncing and hopping on to the kitchen floor, only to be pounced upon by my mother, who regarded her concrete floor as a sacred no-go area, and also the two fireside stone hobs that glistened with snow-white lime wash. She would immediately say to my father, '*A Sheáin, déanfaidh sé báisteach; caithfidh tú an simné a ghlanadh*'; to which he'd reply, '*Tarriceoidh mé scothán tríd amárach*', meaning, 'John we will have rain, you must clean the chimney.' My father would reply, 'I will pull a thorn bush through it tomorrow.'

The masonry of the fireside became a nesting place for house chicks, like grasshoppers they chirped incessantly at the approach of rain. The old cabin was built sometime in the eighteenth century, and lost its rooftree 6th January 1839, the Night of the Big

Wind, when my grandfather and family were forced to shelter under a hedge until daylight.

Another feature of our primitive lifestyle was how our parents used the sun's shadow in the doorway of the house to tell the time of day. It became our sundial, while the sky was clear. Then came the German alarm clock, followed by the American striking clock, reminding us how much we must learn about how to divide and use time.

The exciting impact of modern technology on old voodoos and on all irrational superstition seems to have delivered a death blow to our hitherto ancestral thinking. The *slua sí,* called 'the fairy host', lived in forts and *liosachain.* There were *sprids,* Irish for spirits (not to mistaken for a brand of whiskey), goblins, leprechauns and pookas. The *púca* was a dark foreboding, shapeless spirit while the sprid was a shining brightness. The dark phase of the moon was a perfect setting for all shapes and forms of frightsome figures, scaring the wits out of all kinds of God-fearing early and late Irish Christian peasants. With the advent of electricity things started to brighten up causing the *púca* and *sprid* to vanish into the darkness leaving the Irish countryside cluttered with poles.

The old-time fisherman with his rowboat and sail had an inbred list of beliefs, with regard to the unknown, a list of 'do's' and 'don'ts', such as the misfortune of accosting a 'red-haired Mary' on his way to the fishing pier. Meeting a fox, a hare or a clergyman presaged direful consequences. The whistling sailor was frowned upon, especially in a period of calm: 'Disturb not the sleeping wind lest it might blow a storm.' Internationally, sailors feared to embark or put to sea on Friday the 13th. Locally, the Feast of the Assumption, the 15th of August, was noted for numerous boating accidents and drownings, thus local folk would suspend fishing trips until the jinxed period had elapsed.

The *téitis,* pronounced 'tay-tish', was the Irish name for the 'water sprite'. Phantom boats, the *bad sí,* or 'fairy boat', could be equalled to the spectral apparition of the 'Flying Dutchman', appearing as the wraith of a ship under full-sail, usually spied by mariners caught in storm conditions while rounding the Horn. Such sightings were seen to be a premonition of some tragic event – drowning or shipwreck. A story is told how several people in the townland observed a boat being rowed swiftly and silently towards the shore where the river Inny enters the sea. The description given is of the four oarsmen, bareheaded, wearing white vests or shirts that glistened in the summer sun. As the haymakers watched, the boat and its ghostly crew suddenly vanished into nothingness, giving rise to a spiritual warning of some impending tragedy. Some short time after this odd appearance a locally organized horse race took place on the south bank of the Inny Strand. That evening a sad happening occurred – four men from the locality drowned while fording the River Inny.

During my years as a fisherman, sometimes on a long lonely vigil at night, I have observed many multicoloured sunsets and dawns, some cold and dreary, others warm and rosy. I have witnessed starry, frosty nights with fiery constellations blazing in the vault of heaven, and contemplated the Milky Way, *Bóthar Bó Finne*, with billions of other worlds rolling forever in the mysterious infinity of space.

This poem I have composed specially in memory of my mother, who so graciously helped the neighbours to enjoy each storytelling session by making all of us feel comfortable and welcome.

## The Last Story

*When at last*
*The play of life has ended,*
*The lids droop weary*
*And the curtains start to fall,*
*Dear Mother*
*Tell me one last*
*Bedtime story,*
*Ere slumber deep*
*My senses will enthral.*
*Your soothing words*
*Shall evermore enshroud me*
*And chorus with the Angels*
*When they call.*

# II

*Between the Tides*

## SEA KELP, ROCK POOLS, BEACHES AND STRANDS

The ebbing and flowing of the tide – called the ebb and the flood, and caused by the gravitational pull of the sun and the moon – has two high tides and two low tides in each lunar day, perpetually ebbing and flowing, leaving two tide marks, one high-water and one low-water mark. Within the tidemark can be found an array of marine life and a feeding ground for many of the seabirds I mention. The exposed rocks of *Rinn Dubh*, 'the black reef', could at low tide be described as an undersea garden full of different sea plants and rock pools of clear green seawater, where rock ling and bull-horned blennies dart for cover beneath the seagrass, the bladderwrack and 'the drowning man's seastrings'. One part in particular was my favourite, where the sweet, edible sea dulse grew in profusion. The red fronds would turn a bluish-green in July – then it had less iodine content. When dried to become crisp in the sun it had an appetizing salty flavour. It is widely used as something to whet the appetite. The long searods, each with its clump of red-brown kelp for a crown, were exposed in thousands like a forest of miniature tropical plants, each searod rooted firmly to the rock. Other species of brown kelp are called ribbon and stripe, having a shorter leg than the searod.

The dark bladderwrack, with short root, is branched like a fuchsia bush, containing numerous air blisters like modern 'bubble foam', which perhaps were provided by nature to help it stand upright in the water – clever fellow, this nature. How he seals the air into all those little sacs is beyond me.

Several other sea plants grow on the *Rinn Dubh*. Carrageen Moss is to be found in large quantities; having a rich mineral and medicinal content, jellies and beverages are made from it. Another interesting seaweed we call 'Mermaid's Hair', or 'Tresses'; in Irish we knew it as *Triopall na Muirmhná*. It grows in separate skeins from one root, having long, thin, hair-like strings.

One pond in the shelter of the reef had a dense growth of sea laces, or drowning strings, we called *rachacha*, making it impossible to row a boat or swim in that section. Some strings would measure eight feet long, thin and tough as shoelaces and firmly anchored to the seabed, making a dense carpet of hundreds of thousands of drowning strings.

The reddish-purple coloured minor dulse, which sprouts in little bunches – each little plant with a tiny blue mussel clinging to its root – grows best in shelter and among the baby mussels. When dried in the sun it is sweet and tangy and is sold commercially, especially to beer drinkers.

Among the other salt-water rock plants is the dark, glossy *sleaidí*, and also the shiny brown *sliúcán* (which if boiled and eaten with butter makes a tasty and wholesome dish). Both marine plants are tidal and need exposure to air and light between tides. *Sleaidí* and *sliúcán* are both Irish names, the English and Latin versions are 'sea-lettuce', *ulva lactuca,* and 'laver', *porphyra.*

One small plant, which grows only about two inches high, and is brown, branched and brittle, we called *Seán te,* or 'hot John', because of a hot sweet taste. Others say it is a species of agar-agar. There are many other forms of kelp: two-tufted short searods, serrated yellow ribbon kelp, broad stripe whipleg kelp. All these forms we used to manure our potato and vegetable plots. When mixed with farmyard manure they made excellent fertilizer.

The seabirds came in flocks to search for food in the strand by the *Rinn Dubh*, and still do. The grey heron would stand as still as a statue of slate-grey stone gazing into that part of the rock pool it had chosen, waiting for an elver to appear.

A large flock of sand larks called dunlins, and several tide waders called sandpipers, little strand hens, greenshanks and turnstones, curlews and whimbrel, feed on the table of the tides, when there is a scarcity elsewhere. The exposed sand banks and mudflats offer a variety of food – small crabs, sand eel fry, sand-hoppers, sea mice, sandworms and green lugworms. The curlew and the sand-piper can insert their sharp, pointed bills to a depth of three or more inches into soft sand to drag out sandworms. Many of the smaller waders are migratory to north or south, and numerous in name and size, varying also in colour: redshanks, greenshanks, little stints, turnstones, that work on shingle beaches at night, feeding on sand-hoppers and sand fleas. Equipped with strong stubby beaks, they flip over flat stones of considerable size.

Hidden beneath the fronds of kelp in the rock pools there dwells a variety of marine life; green edible shrimp will jerk-swim for cover, leaving only their long hair-like antennae barely visible in the sea growth. I loved to grab a large one, and after mercifully disjointing it I would eat the tail section. Raw shrimp is nutritious and excellent to eat, so is escallop and razor clam. Boiling, I think, destroys the taste. I recommend we go back a little. After all, the man who ate the first blackberry took a chance. Pardon my digression – back to the pool.

We might see a large pink sea-urchin, cunningly hidden beneath a rock shelf, while several smaller edible purple urchins are in various stages of growth, some baby button size, some large as and the same shape as spinning tops, some as big as goose eggs. In the pool also we find three or four different species of crab – the green-backed or *portán glas*, 'the velvet back', and the *luthóg*, the 'rowing' or 'swimming' crab which has flat hinged toes it can use as oars, like the 'freshwater boatman'. The hermit crab is seen to scramble along taking its house on its back, usually an empty whelk shell. The large spider crab will keep to the deeper pools, so also the large red edible. Periwinkles and whelk winkles, also small bright yellow winkles, and striped mother-of-pearl, abound in the pools. In the gravel-bottomed rock pools can be found the smooth-shelled oval cockle, also the round, rough, serrated cockle which make delicious chowder.

The *circín trá*, or 'little hen of the strand', is Irish for the sanderling, sand-lark or the dunlin. I often wonder if the little bird takes time to rest or sleep. Night and day I have watched it run nearly as fast as it can fly along by the lip of the wave where the sea joins the sand, running in short fast spurts and uttering its clear sweet short pleasant stuttering whistle, as notes played on a dulcimer. An old Irish proverb says, 'The sandpiper can only feed on one beach at a time.' – *Ní féidir leis an ngobadán an dá thrá a fhreastal.* The *gobadán* in this case is the sandpiper, seapie, oystercatcher or redshank; in stormy weather they move inland to get earthworms.

Rock oysters are found firmly fastened to flat rocks; the under shell is completely flat and cemented by nature as though rock and shell are fused and welded in one. The top shell is curved gently upward, like an overturned saucer, the inside having a glossy mother-of-pearl glaze; they are not edible and have very little fish or body. I tried eating one but found it had a bitter flavour. They are not easily found; they grow in perfect alignment with their natural surroundings, nature providing a perfect camouflage. Common limpets – *bairneach* in Irish – are plentiful on the *Rinn Dubh.* Pyramid limpets and flat limpets called 'Chinese hats' are both edible – when boiled in a stew, limpets make an excellent soup. Shells of limpets, mussels, cockles and winkles are still being uncovered by the bulldozer in the excavation of building sites close to the shore wherever the midden heaps of old dwellings existed, providing proof that the poor Irish peasantry during the Famine years availed of this shellfish for survival.

What other life forms do we find in the rock pool? – sea anemones, very much like cow teats attached to the submerged rocks, some very beautiful and varied colours, red, blue, pink, with an array of pastel colours on the hair-like fringes and tentacles with which they capture the micro-organisms of plankton. I do not know what science has discovered regarding this form of life. The Irish term that was used in reference to it was *bod lice,* meaning 'the rock phallus'.

Starfish are so numerous – they are found on the floor of the ocean, at great depths, on the sands of the shallow seashore, in the rock pools of *Rinn Dubh* and, may I say, almost everywhere. Too many starfish clinging to a lobster pot or a net will immediately give warning to a fisherman that he is operating on what is termed 'hungry ground'. The old fishermen called it *talamh gan beatha,* meaning 'a place devoid of the fruits of life'. The most common starfish is the five-pointed (echinoderm), five flat pointed legs radiating from a central disc. Only on two occasions did I find the sun starfish in the trawl. The central body is a round flat disc, bright yellow, and twelve flat legs of paler yellow. Starfish are very brittle – when dry they become like pieces of dried lime. The species are so plentiful and multicoloured, they contribute to the sedimentation of the oceans. One species of rough, spiny, grey-blue five-tentacled starfish, the legs of which are sometimes ten inches long, tapering to a point. The creature will wrap itself, octopus-like, around a piece of fish bait in a lobster pot. It is also known to smother escallops, depriving them of oxygen. It is a denizen of the kelp floor of the sea. It has thousands of light, pink-coloured, pimple suckers on each arm. I often examined it to find evidence of eyes but on finding no evidence, the eyes must be, I presume, a television screen in its brain, which shows a clear picture of a lobster pot and juicy bait hanging therein.

One rock near *Rinn Dubh* deserves special mention. It is called *Carraig an eascú* – 'Rock of the eel'. The eel in question is the conger. During Famine years a conger eel would be considered manna from heaven. Only on a very low watermark would the rock be exposed. I always found it to have one tenant, or more, in residence, sometimes a lobster or red edible crabs. Conger is not eaten locally, and is not regarded as having a very high commercial value; it is also considered the bane of the lobsterman, wrecking, devouring and wreaking havoc on his gear. Only on very rare occasions did we take the electric eel in our trawl. A near cousin to the conger, it wears a necklace of raised red lumps around the base of the gills and later, in the City Aquarium, New York, I read an information display-panel that said the electric eel could emit a static electric shock powerful enough to immobilize a horse. The eel we captured had its storage batteries weakened from being dragged with the trawl net along the sea floor for a considerable period of time. It still gave shock enough to sting.

# ROCK CLAMS AT *TRÁIGH FRAISCE*

The beach at Boolakeel is wide open to the south-western ocean, which stretches to the Gulf of Mexico and thence to Pine Head, Maine, the pristine, unpolluted water, cleansing and purifying the old bed of razor clams and piddock which have grown in the area during the memory of man. Each year we would await the great 'red strand of Easter', when the sand banks were exposed.

I would go to the strand of *Tráigh Fraisce* with my father and my sister Sheila, who was two years my senior. As teenagers we loved to accompany him – he was the expert and when arriving at the strand, he would study the oval eye-shape signs on the sand left there by the razor clams underneath, telling us in Irish not to trample the sand where the signs were showing plentiful. The razor clam is very sensitive to vibrations overhead and will quickly pull itself down deeply into the soft sand and disappear. Dad was adept with the spade; he would open a trench by the side of the clam bed, exposing the clams as he dug gently along a wall of falling sand. Sheila and myself kept collecting until our rod basket was full of beautiful green-yellow razor clams and fat blue *brilliocáin*, 'piddocks'. Then Dad would lay his spade on his shoulders, as we turned homeward. Mom always bade us welcome with the words in Irish saying, 'Ye are home from the strand and ye have something good.' – '*Sibh slán ón dtráigh agus rud maith agaibh.*' We also knew that Mom's clam chowder was the best in the world.

May I come back to the *Rinn Dubh* and *Loch an Duilisc*, the pool or little pond, among the rocks where the dulse still grows. Many other marine creatures lurk beneath the shelter of the dulse frond; such as a dark, sausage-like, squirming thing we called a *súire*. Marine biologists tell us this species is blind. From my experience, it can get in and out of lobster pots at ease, and like the spider can exude from its body a white milky sticky thread-like filament. It has many hundreds of yellow pimple suckers underneath and has no bone structure. All things fair, the black *súire* is a harmless fellow – to me, a fisherman, at any rate. I feel I have a lot to learn. Another inhabitant of the rock pool is the 'sea needle', known in Irish as *an snáthaid mhara*, a slender amber-coloured serpent-like fish, sometimes twelve to fourteen inches long, with a body no thicker than a pencil. It has a transparent bugle-end beak, tiny yellow eye-beads, and wavy dorsal fin. Why it will enter lobster pots I do not know as it can only feed on minute forms of plankton.

The colourful dragonet can be found in the depths of the Atlantic shelf at one hundred fathoms, and also in the rock pool on the sea shore; adorned in bright blue blending with buttercup yellow, pastel green and grey stripes, with an underbelly of faded white, it presents a very beautiful array of complimentary colour.

The dragon-fish has a pyramid-shaped head, with nasty needle spines growing from its forehead and from the side of its gills; its dorsal fin is a feathery growth, concealing several needle-pointed spines. Two ferocious glaring green eyes add to its formidable appearance. It is not edible and its sting is poisonous. Usually it measures not more than nine inches in length. Another comrade in the pool is the horn-headed lumpsucker, in Irish called *an deilgín deamhain*, 'the spiny or thorny demon'. But though nature did not endow poor old lumpsucker with handsome features, I'd much rather shake hands with him than his colourful neighbour the dragonet. The lumpsucker has a round disc on its under carriage which it will adhere to its prey.

## DIGGING SAND SPRAT

I will go back some four score years … I was a raw-boned *garsún*, talking, walking, sleeping, eating … twelve years for my coming birthday. My Dad loved the strand and what better place in the full of the moon, when the tide was low, than *boig a chaisleáin*, the sand bank below the old ruined castle on Ballinskelligs Strand. It was there the *scadán gainí,* the sprat-like sand elvers or sand herring, were plentiful. The little silver fish were no more than two and a half inches long. When washed and dried, sprinkled with flour, pepper and salt, fried to a crisp in butter they made a tasty meal. Dad brought a short shovel – he didn't have to use it much. We just danced on the soft sand and this brought the sprats to the surface. I carried a wooden bucket; when this was about half-full of the silver minnows my father said in Irish, '*Tá do dhóthain díobh agat.*' – meaning, 'You have enough.' Nights such as those have a marked chapter in the book of my memory, with moon rays glancing on the soughing wavelets on the strand beneath the old castle, and mingling with the laughing cackle of the sand larks – simple events of beauty that are so hard to erase from the mind.

A small bed of blue mussels grew on the side of the *carraig* where the fresh water from the mountain entered the sea. Mussels were allowed to grow undisturbed when I was a teenager. We did not buy mussels in tins, or in frozen packs. The only occasion my Dad would ask us to get a bucket of mussels was when he ran short of bait for bottom fishing. He would parboil them, making them easy for impaling on the hook. It was good bait for whiting and cod.

## SEA GRASS

Banks of rough shelly sand, where the plain piddock clams grow in abundance, are found in the shallow reaches of Ballinskelligs Harbour. Most of this area is covered with a growth of green-blue sea grass, called in Irish *muirleog,* not unlike our rye grass; the roots are sweet and edible. At least we as youngsters chewed them and the experiment only whetted our appetites for more.

Where the *muirleog* is found growing in profusion on the sea floor, there too will be found the many species of fish found to inhabit this healthy environment. The ballan wrasse and gunner, also called connor fish – in Irish *ballaigh* – live and breed in the sea grass floor. Some take on a bright blue-green shade, others remain a light brown, while still others are bright and speckled.

Plaice love to hide beneath the cover of the *muirleog,* where they grow fat on succulent lugworms, and browse on young clam tips. The plaice, sand dab and black sole will dig in and lie completely covered; except for tip of nose and two beady eyes barely visible, black sole will cover itself with an inch or more of sand. Codling love the sea grass floor, because of the small green crabs they find among the stalks, in addition to the rays and skate, especially the thorny-backed species.

Lobsters are hermits by nature and like plenty of cover. I have set lobster pots and have found many in the sea grass. Of course escallops shelter and breed there as well. A most likely place to set a trammel net is in the shallow sea grass in the shelter of a point near the shore.

## THE GREY SEAL OF *CUAS DUBH*

The smell of sea kelp in the caves, when the tide is low, especially on a warm summer's day, is reminiscent of the scent of iodine. The smell of tar, the smell of salt fish, the smell of frothy brine, churned into little floating islets of foam, with the gaping indentation of *Cuas Dubh,* 'the Black Cave', between the awesome grandeur of Bolus and Duchalla headlands – enough nostalgia to make an old fisherman remember.

It was here that we anchored our boat while lobstering in seasonal weather. The different smells of the sea were all to be found in the Black Cave. The different smells become stronger, being seaborne across thousands of miles of ocean. Gone was the scent of the meadow, the flowers, the peat and the heather. Instead, the wind, blowing usually from the west, brought new and stronger odours of plankton and fish oil arising from schools of different fish, such as mackerel, herring, pilchard and sprat.

The towering cliff-face above *Cuas Dubh*, where once the golden eagle looked down from its eyrie, is now alas forsaken; but that was in my grandfather's time, when eagles were common birds of prey in South Iveragh. It is still home to the peregrine hunting hawk, which I have watched swoop like a thunderbolt through a stand of whimbrel, leaving some dead and maimed among the rock pools of *Rinn Dubh*.

But *Cuas Dubh* was never a lonely place, the fulmar constantly floating with phantom-like weightlessness overhead, as if free from all gravitational influence, with outstretched silver wings forever wheeling close to its nesting place. Then, the huge flagstone, which had lain like a smooth piece of porcelain in a show case, which weighed many, many tons, became the target of a fiery bolt from heaven during a spectacular thunderstorm, splitting it like a broken star, with a ponderous hammer-blow of natural energy. Yes, it was never lonely; it was inhabited by that very intelligent animal, the grey Atlantic seal. Where and when a fisherman may set a net, the seal will surely find it, if anywhere near its own territory, and by this I mean, near to their own homes. These homes are called in Irish *na dallóga* – underwater caverns whose openings are beneath the sea surface, often with vast, high-roofed chambers inside, or perhaps a succession of rooms. I have often listened to the eerie wail or mating lament of the grey seal echoing through the vaulted ceilings of their spacious dens – a spine-chilling call in the quiet of the night, like a dirge of the damned from the depths of the netherworld.

The seal has a very keen sense of hearing and observation, perceptive of the fisherman's movements. It can propel itself rocket-like through the water at an astonishing speed, following the fisherman far to sea, miles from land, and always at the fisherman's expense, gorging and cramming itself until it can eat no more. I have watched the herd bask under the midday sun on a flat rock the old fishermen called *Leac an Róin*. Some of the great bulls attain huge proportions, presenting a very unwieldy appearance on land, so different from the acrobatic agility they display in water.

We are told the seal possesses a large brain – hence its intelligence – and that it is easily trained from infancy. The seal is also very curious, becoming fascinated with music, especially that of the button accordion. Many old tales in Irish folklore, as well as tales in European folklore in general, make reference to the seal as being enchanted and having a human as well as an animal dimension.

An old man told me a story, which was of course folklore from the mythical past, but related in the musical language of the Gael it sounded much better than I can relate it in English.

An old couple, Tomás and his wife Eibhlín, lived by themselves in a small *bothán* by the sea, near Oisín Strand. The little house had but one window in the front wall, facing the ocean, and but one door in the back wall, facing the hill – the reason for not having a front door being that the house was perched precariously close to the cliff top, and when storms arose the surf would wash against the front wall, so naturally the designer of the building decided it was perfectly logical that the door be at the rear. The reason why the residence was built on the cliff edge was that it was commonage and deemed free from landlord rack-rents and of course, planning restrictions, architects' fees, etc.

Now, having successfully dodged the taxman, Tomás and Eibhlín lived by catching fish in the harbour. They kept bees in the thatch of the roof, and brewed a sweet beer from the tips of the purple heather, which when mixed with honey, created a surpassing soothing experience in all who supped it.

The recipe for the brew (the old man told me) was given to them by tourist friends of theirs who had visited Ireland, and called themselves Don and Eanna and Skeine. He was of the opinion their surname was Milesian, or Fir Bolg, or some cross name like that.

One day while Eibhlín was walking by the beach collecting *smidiríní raice* for the household fire, she found a young pup seal, barking and wailing plaintively as if it was an abandoned child. Eibhlín was filled with pity for the motherless waif, so she took it home and fed it fish and honey and in no time at all the creature became very domesticated. Tomás would sing the beautiful elegy of the drowned fishermen, '*Carraig Aonair*', and each time the young seal would chorus the air of the song in perfect mournful lament.

Eibhlín would remonstrate with Tomás, saying there was something supernatural in the reaction of the seal to the song – perhaps he was the reincarnation of some drowned fisherman. Now Tomás and Eibhlín, having no children of their own, decided they would give their adopted pet a name. Of course, adoption law was not that strict in those days; neither was there any children's allowance. The Brehon Law did not impose tax on pets, and as Tomás and Eibhlín were only late converts to the Christian faith, and had taken on Jewish names, they had no difficulty in calling their newly adopted pet Donncha. The name Donncha Donn was later used by a high king of Ireland, and also by a son of King Brian Boru. It was a pre-Christian name meaning 'the dun' or 'the brown one'.

In a short time the pet seal answered to his new name. Even when he wandered as far to sea as the Gownach Rock, Eibhlín would only stand on the cliff top and call his name aloud – 'Donncha!' It was a sight to watch her pet come streaking home through the sea, shaking the salt water from its flippers to greet her at the water's edge.

The days lengthened into years. Tomás and Eibhlín were very, very happy. Donncha went when and wherever they would go, nearly always on fishing trips. Their pet became the joy of their simple lives. He would balance on his flippers and tail when he wanted to communicate. They knew when he was thirsty, hungry or wanted to sleep.

Then one night their happiness was rudely shattered, when the body wind of a giant hurricane came storming in from the Bull Rock. It was a terrible night; the little house on the cliff top shook and shuddered as each whirling gust tried to rend it apart. Booming broken breakers crashed like thunder beneath the cliff, sending the broken surf high into the night sky. Tomás and Eibhlín were praying when they heard what resembled a human call coming from the body of the storm. Eibhlín, becoming frightened, crossed herself and said, 'Tomás, don't you hear? What was that?'

'It is a human cry,' said Tomás, 'maybe a shipwreck. I will go to the beach – someone is in trouble.'

This time the call came much louder, nearer and clearer – 'Hey Donncha!' to be repeated over and over until it reached the back door of the little house – always the same singing voice, 'Hey Donncha! Hey Donncha!'

Just as Tomás was about to go out into the tormented night, the pet seal spoke. 'I am Donncha. It is my brother Tadhg who has searched the ocean for me – I must go to him.'

Tomás and Eibhlín opened the door in fear and trembling, and with heavy hearts watched their much-loved Donncha disappear into the storm, never to return.

# III

## *Bird-Life*

# THE GANNET

When asked too many questions regarding bird life, a Gaelic poet, becoming annoyed, answered: '*Ní bod gaoithe mé, ná sciathán leathair go bhfaghinn duit cúntas ar Éanaibh Reatha*,' meaning, 'I'm not a kestrel nor a bat (wing of leather), that I can give knowledge about birds of feather.' Be that as it may, I will try to bestow on you, my lay brothers and sisters, the little I know about out feathered friends of the sea. Few fishermen are without some knowledge of seabirds. Each day they are seen in company with them trying to eke out an existence, sometimes frugal and difficult in stormy weather.

Fishermen are keen to observe the movement of different seabirds and how they congregate in numbers in a certain area. More often than not, they are the telltale token that vast schools of fish move beneath the surface, especially schools of herring, mackerel, pilchards, sprat, etc. The trained eye of the fisherman will also judge the direction in which the fish is moving. Despite new technology, we should not ignore our feathered friends who live beside us in the same vineyard, 'the Kingdom of the Wave'.

The first of our many seabirds that I wish to present to you is the gannet, or solan goose, of which at least 30,000 make their home on Little Skellig, a rock situated nine nautical miles west of Bolus Headland, Co. Kerry. The great bird is visible to the eye, when the sky is clear, at a distance of two or three miles, usually hovering over the schools of fish, high above the waves when the fish swim deep, and flying low when the fish are near the surface. Cruising at an altitude of more than two hundred feet, it will suddenly close its wings and plummet from the blue, entering the ocean depths like a spear cast from the heavens. Nature provides the gannet with a system of air sacs around the base of the neck that fill automatically, acting as shock absorbers to take the energy from the impact of the dive. The solan goose – its name is Scandinavian – is a ferocious, daring bird, full of muscle and staying power. It can cruise above the water for hours, wheeling high above its prey, gliding on outstretched, rigid pinions. The white of its plumage stands out when seen against a background of blue sky or the green of the ocean, becoming like some astral white light glinting in the sunshine.

In early spring the gannet will prepare for nest building. It will forage far into shoreline estuaries to collect sea-laces and floating strings of bladder wrack, to line its nest with. The nest can best be described as having only the semblance of a place to hatch out their young. The goose gannet will produce one egg in March, of bluish grey-green colour, speckled with little black and brown dots, the dots sparsely arranged at intervals, forming a beautiful, ornate design. The parent birds sit on the egg for a period of six weeks, relieving each other at intervals, faithfully covering the egg with their wide webbed paws, something not peculiar to any other seabird. The newly hatched chick is black as coal and is continuously fed by both birds for a period of not less than three months; by such time the chick will resemble a fluffy ball of fat. The method of feeding is by regurgitation – the parent bird will insert its beak into the gullet of the young chick, leaving it some partly digested food (usually fish). The feeding continues incessantly during daylight hours.

Scientists tell us that the chicken will take five years to become fully grown, and that the adult life span can be as much as fifteen years. Judging from my own experience it will take the chick three years to lose its black plumage, except for the extreme wing tips, which remain black for life. When the fat chick is more than three months old and can waddle unsteadily on its webbed feet, it will be coaxed and nudged over slabs and ledges until it finally reaches the sea. Sometimes it may float off on a retiring wave, or fall flop into the sea from an overhanging cliff-face.

Once in the water, the parent birds in some mysterious way will spirit their offspring clear of the surf-bound shore, out into the free ocean currents. From now on it will be starvation diet. It is not known whether the chick is entirely left on its own, to live off its own fat, until lean enough to become airborne, or perhaps fed occasionally. I have seen chicks that appeared lean and scraggy make several attempts at take-off before finally soaring into the blue.

Before the couple starts nest building, they enjoy a long courting season, and can be seen like human lovers with necks and wings entwined. This is like a long honeymoon period before they mate, and long after their offspring is reared, this amorous display of lovemaking continues.

It was a very special day in my life, when I climbed the dangerous, lofty cliff-face of Small Skellig. Looking back, I have reason to believe how foolish I had been, since I had no experience or training in climbing, but was only imbued with a burning desire to view the habitat of the great gannetry at close quarters. Nor was I disappointed in an adventure that gave me excitement, pleasure and overwhelming wonder. The raucous din of thousands of bird-calls filled the air, shutting out even the noise of the surf in the caves below. The overwhelming smell of guano, lime and calcium through the salt air, seemed to permeate the gentle sea breeze. This was the effect caused by the accumulation of bird droppings over the centuries – fragments of rotting fish, eggshells, dead birds and feathers also filled many deep veins in the slatey rock structure of the island.

Some parts of the nesting colony were very dense, and here I observed the birds constantly pecking at each other, but never in actual combat; others squabbled over nesting material. Every square foot of one flat area seemed to contain a parent bird and chick. The most amazing feature was how each gannet found its own square foot of space within what seemed to me a maze of confusion.

The birds will not attack a human if one stands still and completely ignores their presence. I had received this piece of good advice from a qualified bird woman – I found it worked perfectly.

Gannets swallow their fish head first, and consume many times their own weight. When diving, the bird will utter a hoarse warning cry – '*krake, krake, krake*'. Scientists tell us the gannet once had a tongue and can no longer taste. All I can say is I have examined dead birds and find that a part of the tongue is still there, the front part not pointed, it is very short and straight across – perhaps it is the root. It also has nostril apertures. It probably is speaking from its stomach. The bird has many different sounds. No doubt the bird may be equipped with taste buds and all faculties for survival. I have found drowned gannets entangled in fishing nets, their length 34-37 inches, wing span 19-20 inches. My father referred to the gannet in Irish as *An Súlaire*. Today it is called *gainéad* or *ogastún*. The great beak is likened to a sharp, pointed dagger, and is slate blue in colour, as are its webbed feet.

In summer gannets are found from Iceland to Canada, from the Faeroes to Rockall, from Skellig Michael to Land's End, and the Azores.


## THE CORMORANT

This diving bird has many other names than that of cormorant, such as 'black hag', 'sea raven', 'shag' or *seaga* in Irish. Shakespeare mentions the black hag in some writings; the bird looms up in other classics as an omen of dark foreboding. According to scholars, the bird has been with us for millions of years going back to the reptilian era (Phew! – who wants to be around that long?), and furthermore, it has changed and survived during that period. It has a special ability, which other species do not have, to show its head and neck above water while keeping its body submerged: nature's equivalent to the periscope of a submarine.

The cormorant will only nest in special, open caves with high ceilings and tiers of rocky shelves, where the churning seas of a storm will not disturb them. Clad in a dark coat, with a sheen of green and purple gloss mixed with wing and back feathers, on dry and windy days the bird will stand upright on a rock for hours on end. It will be seen with outstretched wings, preening, air-drying and oiling its feathers from the skin glands; owing to long submerged periods, it is most important that the plumage be impervious to water.

Cormorants' nests are usually dirty and foul smelling, composed of a yearly accumulation of dried and damp seaweed; very little land vegetation, dried grasses or twigs, are seen to be used by the cave-dwelling species.

The cormorant is found to nest in trees in some countries, and occasionally here in Ireland. The Japanese have trained cormorants to fish for trout in their rivers. Three or four long, white, slender eggs, adorned with little streaks of blue, are laid in late March. The new chicks when hatched resemble young mice, devoid of feather or fur, just a greyish pink flesh-colour. The method of feeding is the same as that of gannets, by regurgitation. The bird has small green eyes of a luminous shade, and an evil-looking hooked beak coming to a sharp downward point; its webbed feet are dark green.

The green cormorant is the oldest and the smallest of the species and wears a crest of green feathers similar to that of a green crested plover, a decoration that the other relations do not have.

The largest of the species is the white-breasted shag, which is seen to travel inland to streams and rivers, where they freeload on salmon and trout fry. The shag family are not so much cave dwellers, but like to nest on the inaccessible ledges of high, cliff-faced headlands. Cormorants can search for food very close to the seafloor. I have found them trapped and drowned within lobster pots and entangled in sunken nets. Cormorants can stay submerged for prolonged periods and can withstand water pressures of several fathoms. A colony of cormorants are still to be seen, as I saw them when I was only nine years old, almost eighty-six years ago. *Cuas a tSeaga* is still the same, the birds that emerged from the secret womb of time still survive, and keep that secret well.

# THE PUFFIN

Puffin Island is situated close to the headland of Moyrisk, or *Mao-raisc,* on the northern arm of St Finan's Bay, near Ballinskelligs. It is now a bird sanctuary.

The puffin, a member of the auk family, measures about twelve inches in length and seven inches wingspan outstretched. The bird has many names: 'sea parrot', 'clown pope', and *cánan dearg* and *puifín* in Irish. Its ponderous beak seems out of proportion to the rest of its face, giving it a clown-like appearance. The beak will increase in size during a long spring mating season, the varied and beautiful colours becoming more pronounced and vivid, bright orange mixed with red and blue stripes; this is more apparent in the male, who seems to show off his gaudy finery, while his wife's plumage is drab in comparison. The colours remain until winter, when a portion of the heavy beak is shed in October, a process repeated by Mother Nature at the advent of the next mating season.

The body of the bird is rotund and plump; its little webbed feet and shanks are of a red flesh-colour hue, and its back feathers are a grey mouse colour with a neck-collar of the same above a white breast. A puffin will assume to the beholder a pose of authority, like that of an admiral; it will stand on a ledge for long periods, gazing out to sea, seemingly indifferent to its immediate surroundings.

Late in spring the hen will produce one large white egg, to be hatched underground, safe from the prying eyes of the arch marauder, the great black-backed gull. The underground nest site is usually a narrow tunnel expertly constructed beneath a mound of peat-like soil, the residue of many centuries of decaying sea pinks, also the yellow and white sea samphire. With only its great strong beak, short muscular wings, short legs and little sharp-toed, webbed feet as tunnelling tools, the little bird must be commended for its engineering skill, so deeply ingrained in its nature. A disused rabbit burrow can also become a ready-made nesting place. The summer is nearly at hand by the time the young chick breaks the shell in the darkness of his underground cradle.

The little infant is not endowed with handsome features at birth. I found young chicks on the Skelligs covered with black hairy fluff, each with an ugly beak, like a crook on a wall. But the old saying in Irish puts it aptly: *Is fada dho ráite gur geal leis an bhfiach dubh a ghearcach fhéin* – 'The raven thinks its own chick is pure white.' In a short time, the black plumage will change to greyish white; by that time the fledgling will be able to waddle towards the daylight near the entrance of the tunnel. There, it will be fed tiny silver sprats and sand eels by both parents.

Puffins do not dive from the sky but submerge and swim beneath the surface for long periods, searching for sprats and minispecies. I have watched puffins flying towards the Skelligs from far out to sea, their beaks laden with silver sprats. Young puffins are spirited to the sea on moonlit nights – how this is done remains a mystery to me.

Puffin Island is an undisturbed sanctuary where birds can live and breed without much interference from humans. The island has no man-made landing place, with only a few sheep kept by local farmers from the mainland. Rabbit warrens and banks of turf are plenty, sea-thrift abounds in profusion, making an ideal nesting-place for several species of seabirds, such as auks, shearwaters and petrels.

The north side of the island is home to the guillemot family on the high shelves of the barren rocky cliff-face, where fulmar petrels and soot-coloured skuas patrol the wild and windswept air-space above, while clusters of lesser gulls, screaming terns and complaining kittiwakes dispute their share of mini-sprat and plankton thrown up by the crashing surf beneath.

# THE ROCK PIPIT

In Irish the pipit is called *an beagéan carraige*, meaning 'little bird of the rocks'. It is also known as *riabhóg chladaigh*, 'the stripy one on the shore'. The meadow pipit seems to be exactly the same bird as the rock pipit, one of nature's enigmas. I will not even attempt to find myself a suitable answer; both species are so similar, the difference is almost indiscernible. They have the same plumage and flight pattern, and build the same-shaped nest, using the same withered grasses, weaving in some hair and feathers, except that the rock pipit may use a dried sea string occasionally.

Scholars make the suggestion that some millions of years ago the pipit family suffered a severe disagreement, causing the flock to split up. One part took to the seashore, the other part stayed in the meadow. What the disagreement was about the scholars do not tell us. Perhaps it came about at the reading of the will, when bird property was being disposed of. However, they still sing the same ballads. Some say the rock pipit's voice is sweeter. In my youth I heard the meadow pipit being referred to as *Seánín na lathaí*, meaning 'Johnny of the gutter'. Other names for the meadow pipit are *riabhóg mhóna, banaltra na cuaiche, fuiseog mhóna* and *riabhóg bheag*.

I had found the pipit's nest in the meadow many a time, but later on I was taken aback to observe the little fellow ballet-dancing on the wild spume and spray-soaked rocks of Bolus Head. Of course this was not the meadow pipit I had taken it for – it was the other disgruntled part of the family, the rock pipit. The blithesome creature could be likened to some superactive flying phantom, full of unending energy, constantly running, searching and collecting the minute particles called plankton.

A stormy day is best to enjoy the antics of this elusive feathered artist of the flying trapeze. No matter how high the breakers come combing, tumbling and foaming over his rocky domain, he is never found trapped or injured. The nimble 'water sprite' will always rise higher than the blown sea spray. The little bird will follow the receding wave with perfect confidence and composure, feeding on the micro-morsels washed ashore from nature's bountiful larder. One would assume the little mite is only mocking the fury of the elements and the strength of the mighty ocean, and it cannot be compared with other seabirds.

The rock pipit has not the appearance of a fisherman, nor ever will, yet it wins its daily bread between the tidemarks of the wave. It is pitiful to watch a creature so frail, with weak, thin shanks, wading in shallow rock pools in company with other seabirds.

True to their family, agreement or disagreement, the rock pipit will build its nest on the very edge of the cliff top, where the last blades of grass curl down from land overhead. I happened on a nest by mere chance while walking close to the edge of a stony clay cliff. The nest was carefully concealed below the meadow line, yet under the lip of the cliff. It was woven from withered sand-dune grass and some tiny fluffy feathers; it was cosy and cup-shaped, well-shielded from the rain and wind by tufts of sea pinks and bunches of white sea-thrift, mingling with other grasses. White sea-thrifts are sometimes referred to as 'dead men's flowers' because of their brittle stems. Climbers must not grasp them for support.

The nest contained four smoky, grey-green, small eggs with a rusty hue at the extreme ends. At the time, I did not recognize the nest – maybe another meadow pipit's nest, so commonplace in the locality? It was a beautiful work of art on the edge of the Atlantic, perfected by nature's insistence that future propagations of the species might survive – the superb cosy home of the undaunted little waif I have the privilege to describe, and may I add, the excellent fisher, who scorns the fury of mighty Mannanán, little fisher of the rocks, *an beagéan carraige.*

# THE STORM PETREL

'Little Peter' (*Peadairín*) who walks on the water, phantom of the storm. This is the storm petrel, whose cloak is black as coal, a harmless creature, never welcomed by sailors, even to see, and unthinkable that the bird should come aboard: harbinger of storm and misfortune – a bad omen. Many superstitious mariners believe that the little black witches revel in the vortex of an Atlantic hurricane; that is because the bird can be seen anywhere on the far reaches of the ocean, a thousand miles from any nesting place. Little Peter seems to virtually walk on the crest of an approaching billow of brine, scooping up minute droplets of rich fish oil and plankton.

The petrel resembles a species of swallow or black butterfly and is called 'Mother Carey's chickens', or 'Laura of the ocean'. In Irish it is called *an guardal* and again *briochtóg na mara*, 'witch of the sea'. Other names include *gearr róide* and *gearr úisc*.

While many other species of petrels exist, the storm bird is the smallest. Years ago, when British steam trawlers fished off the south-west coast of Kerry, and fish was plentiful, the ships would shelter in Ballinskelligs Bay. The captains and crew were generous and would give us baskets of scrap fish with which to bait our lobster pots. I remember finding a dead storm petrel among the debris of fish on deck. Being curious to examine it, I held it in my hand as a member of the ship's crew protested most vehemently, 'Do not touch it, boy, it will bring you bad luck.' I immediately cast the creature's mutilated body overboard and asked the seaman if the storm petrel really brought bad luck. He replied, 'Don't ever handle them, boy, them's bad members!' Despite the seaman's warning, I could not bring myself to entertain any superstitious belief that Little Peter was endowed with any magical power which enabled it to stir up hurricanes in the Gulf of Mexico.

Towards the end of spring, the little dusky seafarers decide to obey the inborn call, which is fixed in the creation of all species (When? I do not know – the answer is blowing in the wind). The birds will converge upon their natural habitat, in the local case primarily Skellig Michael, Puffin Island or the Blaskets.

They will faithfully turn homeward, perhaps on a certain date, no matter how far afield, steering an unerring, leisurely course, sleeping, mating and feeding on the broad reaches of the Atlantic. On arriving home they find the old tunnels and retreats, or perhaps will build anew, between fissures in loose stone walls, places difficult to find, and safe from predators. The chick emits a low, hoarse, chirring sound. The nest is that of a sea-dweller, only a few strands of dried grass, a few feathers, a place to keep an egg warm. When June is at hand, one white egg is laid. After that the parent birds are not seen on land in daytime. Under the cloak of night and within the darkness of the burrow the new chick is hatched, fed and made ready to be introduced to the sea. All is prepared under cover of complete darkness, thus avoiding the great black-backed gull, indiscriminate slayer of chicks.

It is not easy to estimate the power of nature, which enables a little bird with matchstick-thin shanks and webbed feet flat enough to enable it stand momentarily on a hillock of brine, or dance disdainfully in the womb of a storm. At times wisping witches are seen to congregate close to land – a telltale warning for local fishermen of foul weather (a 'wisp' meaning a little cluster of petrels, not more than three or four).

The different species of petrel are rare to the North Atlantic. Only once have I seen the fork-tailed petrel in the Skelligs area. The bird is not known to nest in the South Kerry region. Ornithologists tell us that the dusky little wave-dancer can waltz the ocean ballroom from the Hebrides to Rockall, from Rockall to Skellig Michael, from the Scillies to the Azores, from the Falklands to Tierra del Fuego, to finally revel in the spume of the Horn.

Little Peter who walks on the water, your heritage is the vineyard of the vast ocean – long may you survive.

## THE MANX SHEARWATER

A fisherman who is not familiar with following and searching the south-western waters beyond the Skelligs, and from Kerry Head to the Dursey for the dense mackerel schools, will have missed seeing great strings of Manx shearwater or 'mackerel cock'. The bird is referred to in Irish as *púicín gaoithe* or *an chánóg dhubh*. I do not know why the term 'wind fairy' was used, as it is not a bird connected with stormy conditions. I have observed it in most tranquil conditions, in the quiet of eventide in myriads resting on calm waters. It is known to revel in pleasant breezy conditions, but unlike its cousin the storm petrel, it is not a child of the storm.

The flight pattern of the Manx is both a mystery and a beauty to behold; something in its constant undulating movement seems to suggest a bond of rhythmic unison between bird and ocean. It will glide without effort on seemingly rigid motionless wings, up one side of an Atlantic roller, until it reaches the summit of the billow, then balance delicately on the tip of one pinion to slowly roll over to the opposite wing tip, enabling it to glide effortlessly, using the surface air currents which flow between the sea swells to perfect advantage. Without doubt they are the living music of the waves, rising, falling, floating, weaving the self-same tapestry with unerring precision. The mackerel man will welcome flocks of shearwaters near his boat when he is about to cast his nets at twilight, safe in the knowledge that the birds follow the migratory schools of fish.

The mackerel cock comes ashore on Skellig Michael and Puffin Island between March and May. Its beak is narrow and flute-like, ending with a sharp, turn-down hook. I often suffered a tormented sleep while anchored beside the Great Skelligs when lobster fishing. The shearwaters would return to their underground tunnels at dusk, all would be peaceful until after midnight; then would start a plaintive persistent clamour, that of a thousand throats, as if mournfully bewailing their lot. English-speaking people defined the cry as a repetition of the expression 'It was your fault, it was your fault', while Irish speakers interpreted the cry as a repetition of '*Ná dein é, ná dein é*', meaning, 'Don't do it, don't do it.' The outcry would suddenly cease at the first streak of dawn, making the nocturnal host vanish into the morning mists. Now, in my old age, I am convinced that there is a bird language, and a variety of animal talk which man in his supreme position of superiority has failed to decode. Modern technology and communications stop short at the turnstile to the animal kingdom.

The egg of the Manx is white. The young chick is clothed in a shirt of blue-grey down and, for some reason, is in a few days as fat as a lump of butter. The full-grown bird has a black back and a white underbody. A colourful blue stripe divides the white from the black; beak and legs are black. By August, full-grown birds will be able to fend for themselves  and join the main flock in quest of rich micro-organisms in the tide-race of the deep Atlantic. Faithful to their natural instinct, they will return to the coast once again at the approach of winter.

# THE HERRING GULL

Several species of gull frequent the rock-bound coast of Kerry. What more beautiful spectacle than to watch a fishing boat coming to harbour after a successful trip, laden with fish, and the sky around her filled with fluttering white wings of excited seagulls who will faithfully escort in aerial procession until it takes its moorings. The gull family are many, from the grey speckled herring gull to the small black-headed gull, the near all-white, with blue pastel tint on each wing, the grey-brown gull, and the lesser black-backed, a near cousin to the great black-backed, but not as ferocious.

Several of the lesser family fly inland during springtime and autumn, to follow the plough and feed on the rich red earthworms. Gulls have an uncanny way of communication. When a ploughman starts the day, and a sod of soil becomes a furrow, the field may be several miles inland, yet in a short time gulls will converge on the scene, seemingly from nowhere. If a school of sprat or other fish break the surface some miles from land, you will perhaps remember lines from an old poem in our early schoolbooks:

> *out from the shore the seabirds fly*
> *on pinions that know no drooping.*

The sky overhead will immediately fill with clusters of fluttering white-winged gulls.

I am of the opinion that most gulls can see equally well in night-time. Very many years ago we fished for herring with cotton-thread nets, always at night. One would often hear the excited call of the herring gull break the silence of the night when it had discovered a fat herring dangling from the surface meshes of our nets. The call sounded like half-laugh, half-cry – 'Ah ha! I have it! I have it!' In those days birds only spoke their bird talk in perfect Irish, saying, '*Tá agam! Tá agam!*' The chicks of today would never qualify for a five pounds bonus to speak Irish – forgive me if I say they would never be gulled into that.

I often saw a herring gull lift a large hard-shell crab high above flat rocks and let it drop suddenly. This would be repeated several times until the crab burst into fragments, then the bird could make a meal from the crabmeat. Who will say birds can't think?

Gulls nest in secluded areas, places less frequented by man. Their colonies are always crowded, owing to the additional mix of lesser species. Collectors of bird's eggs are known to have suffered serious accident in pursuit of their hobby. Despite what is said about seabirds and slovenly nest building, the herring gull will work laboriously while building a deep-sheltered nest of mostly damp seaweed, grasses, bits of anything, from withered sea pinks, or bracken. Herring gulls are also scavengers, and will follow the wake of a ship for miles, feeding on titbits cast overboard. They are also easily tamed if fed. I got into the habit of feeding a gull from my hand – it became so friendly it snatched my best knife and dropped it into the Atlantic.

# THE GREAT BLACK-BACKED GULL

It is a big bird, king of the gull family, with a beak of bright yellow and a hood, down-turned, with a blood-red stain on the extreme end of the lower bill, giving it the appearance of a bloodthirsty pirate. Only on rare occasions will it nest among other species; even then, it would be considered a most unwelcome neighbour owing to its bellicose temperament.

A bald lump of rough rock separated from the mainland by a gorge-like cleft, wide enough to prevent man's intrusion from the main headland, which is Bolus. The rock, which I mention, is called *Oileán na bhFaoileán*, and is situated between the headlands of Bolus and Duchealla on the Iveragh peninsula, some of the most rugged cliff terrain in the south. It is here the 'Royal Gull' can be seen in a small colony, strutting supreme within the rock-bound turrets of its impregnable fortress.

The black-back is an unmerciful predator of young chicks and eggs of all species except the gannet and the hawk family. All other birds are eternally vigilant during nesting season. I have watched the black marauder stand over the remains of a half-devoured chick, swaying its lowered head and neck from side to side, and with blooded beak, scream a loud clarion call as if telling the bird world that might is right.

The ever-watchful eye of the boastful conqueror has great clarity and a wide range of vision. Not a feather will fall from the sky. Not a pebble will fall from the cliff-face. If a lobsterman discards a crab claw it will never go unnoticed. A piece of barnacled wood is most welcome in stormy weather, when other freeloading takeaways are closed, especially if the barnacles are two or more inches in length. Also a dead body of any kind can be a windfall. At twilight one evening in springtime, it being World War Two, as we were about to set our mackerel gear, we heard the cry of the great gull on our starboard bow, and on moving forward in that direction, to our astonishment we saw the great gull standing sedately on top of the lifting ring of a large floating mine, wailing in a high-pitched note as if to say, 'I am king of the gulls.'

The black-back's nest is only a shelter for the eggs, comprising of pieces of withered seaweed, feathers and other bits of dry material from the cliff-face. No doubt the parent birds see the construction as a work of art and a labour of love, which also applies to all mere mortals – an attempt at home building.

Two or three eggs are produced near the end of May, pale brown in colour, with streaks of a darker brown showing through. The young birds emerge from their shells dressed in shirts of glossy grey down, with spots of black between the shoulders. Very soon, the genes of heredity become apparent in the youngsters who are only some weeks old, yet by now have already turned very rowdy and are given to pecking each other, showing so soon the aggressive characteristics of the parent birds. In their infant stage they are fed from the craw by insertion of the beak where food always awaits them. It will take three to four years for the great gull to become fully developed; by then its legs will be a yellowish red, and its eyes a bright yellow with tiny green flashing pupils.

I have not written in very glowing terms about *an chaobach*. But back in the twenties when herrings were plentiful in Ballinskelligs Bay, hearing the frenzied chuckle of the black pirate in the vicinity of our nets at night – a sure sign that the rogue was having a free serving of fresh herring – was considered a good omen.

# THE LOON

The lonesome call of the loon on a still moonlit night is a sad, wailing cry, reaching a crescendo of sorrowful sound, only to die away suddenly on the night air. On the other hand, come mating time the note of sadness changes to a low musical whistle denoting the desire for continuity, as ordained by forces outside our understanding.

Many, many miles of wild and wide ocean lie between the Arctic Circle and Ballinskelligs Bay, yet a pair of loons will decide to leave the frozen land and climate of their birthplace for the more temperate environs of southern Ireland. They will travel down beyond the Outer Hebrides and Scotland, keeping far from land, guided accurately to their intended landfall by an unerring orientation. In Ireland they frequent tidal estuaries in shallow waters where they feed on small flatfish, sand eels and little crabs. A difficult task for a birdwatcher to get close to this elusive bird – the loon is always seen to place the same gap between itself and its observer, staying submerged for at least ten minutes.

The back and shoulder feathers are a mixture of glossy green and polished dark blue, while the wingtips and breast feathers are a very mottled grey, surmounted by a neck collar with vertical streaks of black. The only time I had the opportunity to examine the loon at close quarters was when, by misadventure, one drowned by getting entangled in one of my fishing nets on the sea floor. I felt sad that such an intrepid voyager from the shores of Greenland should end in a situation akin to that of a human tragedy.

The loon is unable to travel on dry land because its webbed feet are situated to the rear of its undercarriage, but it can pull itself forward with the aid of its wings and by wriggling its body forward. For this reason, the nest is constructed in some sheltered, low, edge area that the bird can enter easily for incubation. Very rarely has it been known for a pair to nest in Ireland. The Irish name for the loon is *lóma*.

The great northern diver is now exposed to a more serious threat to its survival than ever before, that is oil spillage from super tankers, which threatens all marine life.

# THE SKUA

*Tomáisín chac na bhFaoileán,* or in English, 'Little Tommy Gull-shit', is the pirate robber and tormentor of other birds, devouring all unwanted matter. This is a species of the gull family clad in a sombre coat of sooty dark brown giving it an ominous appearance. Fishermen call it the dirty seagull. It can manoeuvre in the air like a falcon – chasing, hunting and harrying the other gulls until they drop a piece of fish, regurgitate or discharge excreta – at the same time uttering a wild, terrifying cry, 'Scheer Scheer', frightening the honest bird to abandon its piece of fish. I have often watched the pirate in pursuit of its repulsive occupation.

Not many pairs are found to nest on the Kerry coast. Only a couple of pairs are seen to nest on *Oileán na bhFaoileán* at present, a barren lump of rock between the wild and majestic headlands of Bolus and Duchealla. The legs and webbed feet are also a dirty brown shade, the bill a wicked, turned-down crook. I never had the opportunity to observe its nesting place at close hand. *Oileán na bhFaoileán* was a dangerous rock to get even a foothold on for the person who wanted to scramble ashore. No wonder that the wild skua had chosen it to be his Bluebeard's Castle.

The chicks and eggs are of the same dreary, drab colour. Nature itself must be blamed for clothing you in such dismal attire, and also for condemning you to piracy, poor Little Tommy Gullshit.

It is interesting to note – according to ongoing Polar research by several countries – that the skua inhabits the South Polar region and can endure and thrive in sub-zero temperatures.

# THE FULMAR PETREL

The fulmar petrel is a beautiful seabird, described by seafaring men in different ways. Some called it *an chánóg liath* – grey puffin, 'mollyhawk', etc., but at the end of the day we are speaking of the great grey petrel called the fulmar. If we accept the conclusion of scientific authority we believe that the fulmar evolved from the same root tree as the puffin and the storm petrel. Be that as it may, when I first was shown the bird and its natural nesting place (by my father John Kirby), I was not interested in its origin or how it had emerged from the primal stygian ooze. I took for granted it was a bird, it was here. I didn't even stop to think how it got here, I just kept on watching the bird. But almost ninety years further on, with less wisdom and more hindsight, I marvel at our scientists who can tell with dogmatic accuracy the origin, the parents, relatives, and even first cousins of little seabirds, who burst from the eggshell of the Big Bang.

The fulmar can still be seen to nest on the northern side of Skellig Michael, where the cliffs rise in lofty grandeur to 600 feet. One would need the skill of an experienced climber to reach the nest or shelf of the site, which is usually built under a canopy of overhanging rock, placed in the most unapproachable position possible. Like a hanging basket roughly made on the outside, with protruding sticks, the interior is much better woven and rounded, with little downy feathers cleverly interlaced with dry withered grass. At least here is a seabird with a more tidy system of house building.

A lone egg is produced in May. The young chicks are fed with oil from plankton and sprat fry; the parent bird will vomit rancid fish oil of a foul, nauseating odour on man or bird who would dare invade the privacy of its sanctuary. The fledgling is allowed to develop a full plumage on the shelf where it is fed and will shake and stretch its wings in preparation for its first flight. The fulmar can display a mysterious mastery of aerobatics, beyond my humble description.

The bird's real home is within the Arctic Circle, but perhaps it will feel more at home up there in the infinite portals of blue space, where its tranquil spirit is seen to float like gossamer webs over a summer meadow.

## THE AUK — AND THE FOLKLORE

The auk family are divided into many relations and cousins. The little auk, dressed like a butler with its white-fronted shirt and black shiny jacket , and the guillemot and the razorbill, are all relatives of the great auk (*falcóg mhór*), which is sadly extinct. The last pair of those great birds was shot in Iceland in 1800, testimony to man's habit of making stupid mistakes based on lack of knowledge. The little auk is closest to the ancestral prototype of the species. The common guillemot is very like the penguin and its favourite nesting places are towering wild headlands, overlooking the ocean, in spots safe from man's intrusion.

The razorbill, *crosán,* is the nearest blood relative to the extinct great auk; entirely black with only one white feather on each wing, it is sometimes referred to as *éan dubh na scadán*, 'the blackbird of the herrings'. The razorbill is easily identified while in flight; it flies in a direct straight line, the beak to the tail of the bird in front.

A folktale in Irish would immediately suggest the belief in reincarnation. The tale was related to me by an old fisherman and Irish storyteller, who would go to great pains to embellish in rich Irish the trappings of his trade.

'It was a hot summer's day – so hot, the sun was splitting the stones. It was like the sun stood still overhead in a clear blue sky, not a cloud white, grey or black from the lip of the ocean to the top of heaven, except one little grey feather which seesawed and floated lazily from right to left downward out of the blue sky and landed in the cup of my palm. The sea was like a dark blue mirror of glass, not a ripple or even a wrinkle on its face. The boat was anchored, Jim was asleep in the bow and the boat had lost all movement. It had lost its soul; it, too, had gone to rest.

'I lay backwards on the thwart – I could not sleep. I fixed and fired the tobacco in my pipe. Gazing up into the blue, I lay soaking solace from the sweet smoke of my burning bowl. Then I saw another little grey feather come seesawing down out of the nowhere of the sky, and reaching out my hand it landed in the cup of my palm. I opened my hand to examine the little grey feather; much to my surprise my palm was empty. Suddenly a cold shiver spread over my whole body. I felt the hair on my head tingle with a thousand pinpricks of 'sleeping griffin' – *codladh grifín*. Then I knew I was being bewitched; a magic spell was making everything confused. I crossed myself. It was then I heard a hollow empty rolling sound mingling with the sharp whirring of wings, approaching from the west. Looking up, I saw several razorbills flying in a straight line, beak to tail except, for one bird trailing a distance behind. It was then the leading razorbill turned its head and shouted in perfect Irish, "*A Mháire Ní Dhálaigh is mór an náire dhuit a bheith chun deiridh*", meaning "Mary Daly it is a great shame for you to lag behind."

'Jim sat up, yawned and rubbed his eyes, saying, "What was that? I thought I heard a voice in the sky! Maybe I was dreaming?"

'I didn't answer him. A dark cloud passed slowly over the face of the sun, it grew cold suddenly, the boat started to sway gently like a child's cradle, the spell was lifted – only a little grey feather wafted to and fro down out of an empty nowhere, to land once more in the cupped palm of my hand.'

This is my story – if it be true let it be so, if it is false let it be so, because it is not I who composed or fashioned it.

The auk family is common to the Iveragh and Kerry coast. In March they will sometimes nest on the naked rock or beneath some boulder-strewn cliff-face. The egg is pear-shaped, with a pattern of brown, yellow and white spots. It is said that no two eggs of the auk family have identical markings. The young chicks will be coaxed and sometimes rudely tossed into the water when scarcely ready to fly; the fledglings would then be about five weeks old. The parent birds would accompany their young, feeding, swimming and diving, while also protecting them from predators, both aerial and marine. I have seen young chicks being pulled under by schools of spike dogfish. I have found little auks blown into the fields by violent winds from the Atlantic.

# THE KITTIWAKE

The first time I had occasion to stay for a set period of time in the close vicinity of the Great Skelligs was the year 1926. I was then twenty years old. Little did I think I would be granted a long and healthy life, time to reflect on what I observed, and a clear memory of the past. Now in my nineties, I will say with the Psalmist – Oh Lord! I love the beauty of thy house, and the place where thy glory dwelleth.

That first trip was not intended to be a sight-seeing tour, but a whole week of hard slogging, hauling, baiting and setting our lobster pots while the weather remained favourable and food supplies lasted. We always anchored our boat in front of Blind Man's Cave, at a place called the south landing. Although I had watched kittiwakes pursue banks of sprat during other fishing trips, this time I had a close-up view, a ringside seat, not to witness a pain-inflicting pugilistic sport, but to watch in wonder a flock of beautiful creatures at home in the roost they had chosen. When they made that choice I do not know – perhaps after the last Ice Age – Brrgh! All in all, it was an excellent roost – they had chosen well.

Blind Man's Cave was sheltered from all sides, an oasis within a bowl of blue-grey towering rock and cliff-face. It seemed as if Mother Nature had inspired her offspring to approve of the site plans she presented to them. The cave itself was shaped like an oval amphitheatre, with tiers of narrow natural shelves on the rocky cliff-face, overlooking the placid pool of sheltered ocean beneath. Every square inch of building space had a kittiwake's nest for generations, the birds resembling white blossoms against the dark background of stone, all sitting on saucer-shaped nests, some sitting solemnly, others with beaks hidden beneath the wing shoulder, peacefully oblivious to the incessant clamour of 'Kittiwake! Kittiwake', the theme song of this feathered choir.

One can't but be impressed by their behaviour and the way they tolerate each other, calling and sharing beakfulls of oily sprat, some standing beside nests full of fledglings, others with necks intertwined, rubbing their heads together and pruning their plumage. The colony is always at different stages of incubation – only when all the young are ready for flight will peace descend.

In the Blindman's Cave only the parent birds will remain to repair old nests for next year's season. Kittiwakes will nest on the sheltered sides of high Atlantic cliffs where ledges for nesting, free from man's interference, are to be found. Colonies also inhabit isolated islands where sprat, krill and sand eel abound in regions as far north as the White Sea.

In August, when the young are trained to eke out an existence, they are seen to fly south into the temperate waters of the Gulf Stream. I have watched kittiwakes from the deck of the S.S. *Dresden*, in mid-Atlantic – this was in January 1929 on my way to the United States of America. It is hard to understand how those weak, gentle birds survive in sometimes-severe weather conditions. Perhaps that is how the Creator ordained that little David should be on a par with Goliath. The kittiwake has lost the hind toe or talon, whether through aeons of evolution or not, I do not know. I am also told that I swung by my tail sometime in that murky past – how fortunate I lost that tail.

The kittiwake has not inherited the rough mannerisms of the gull family, its relative. It remains my choice of seabird – a gentle creature, beautiful lark of the ocean, with plaintive yearning call – 'Kittiwake! Kittiwake!'

# A GLOSSARY OF BIRD NAMES

I have just happened to find a mixed bag of birds I had written into some old papers about fifty or more years ago. At the time I was anxious to find out the Irish names of the many species I could identify in my own locality, with the exception of eagles, which I never saw. I am much indebted to the old men and women who were in their declining years, while I was yet in the bloom of youth. They were so positive and so natural in naming the birds of their neighbourhood. With their help and that of an old book, I found the task comparatively easy.

| | |
|---|---|
| auk | *falcóg mhór* |
| avocet | *camghob* |
| bat | *sciathán leathair, bod dall na hoíche, eitleog, feascarluch* |
| bittern | *bonnán léana, bonnán buí, béicire* |
| blackbird | *londubh, céirseach* (f) |
| chaffinch | *rí rua* |
| chough | *éan na gcos dearg* |
| cormorant | *seaga, cailleach dhubh, broigheall fiach farraige, fiach mara, dubhéan ballaire, gairrfhiach, claimhfhiach* |
| corncrake | *tradhna, gortéan* |
| crow | *préachán* |
|    hooded crow | *préachán liath* |
|    kite crow | *préachán na ceirteach* (of the rags) |
|    raven | *préachán chnámhach* (of the bones) |
| | *préachán an teampaill* (of the graveyard) |
| | *fiach dubh* |
|    scald crow | *préachán na gcearc* (of the hens) |

| | |
|---|---|
| curlew | *cuirliún, crotach, crotach mara, goibíneach* |
| dove | *colm* |
| turtle dove | *féarán fiaigh* |
| duck | *lacha* |
| eider duck | *lacha Lochlannach* |
| merganser | *crannlacha* |
| (red-breasted) | *tumaire rua* |
| dunnock, black-cap | *Donncha an chaipín* (m) |
| | *Máirín an triúis* (f) |
| eagle | *iolar, fiolar* |
| eaglet | *iolarán* |
| golden eagle | *iolar buí, fiolar buí* |
| sea eagle, osprey | *fiolar mara, an iolar ingneach* (of the talons) |
| falcon | *seabhac na seilge* |
| falconer | *seabhacadóir* |
| fieldfare | *liathtráisc, sacán* |
| flycatcher, spotted | *breacán sciobóil, breacán glas* |
| gannet  or solan goose | *ogastún, amhsán, sulaire corróg, gainéad* |
| goldfinch | *buíog an óir, lasair choille, finseog* |
| great northern diver | *lóma, éan glas na scadán* (the green bird of the herrings) |
| grouse, cock | *coileach fraoigh* |
| hen grouse | *cearc fraoigh* |
| guillemot | *falc, cuilín* |
| black species | *éan dubh na scadán, calltóg* |
| | *casgán na long* |
| gull | *faoileann, faoileadán, faoile* (Donegal) |
| | *faoileoig, faoileagán* (Mayo) |
| Kerry black-backed royal gull | *chaobach, faoileann dhromadhuí* |
| jackdaw | *cág* |
| jacksnipe | *gabhairín reo, mionnán aerach, gabhairín oíche, gabhairín bainne* (Clare) |

| | |
|---|---|
| kittiwake | *faireog* |
| lapwing, crested | |
|     lapwing, or green | |
|       plover | *pilibín míog* |
| lark | *fuiseog* |
|    bog or tit lark | *riabhóg na móna* |
|    meadow pipit | *riabhóg mhóna, banaltra na cuaiche, fuiseog mhóna, riabhóg bheag, Seánín na lathaí* |
|    sea lark or rock | |
|      pipit | *bigéan, beagéan carraige, riabhóg chladaigh* |
| linnets or fringilline | |
|    birds | |
|    bog linnet | *gealbhán sléibhe* |
|    grey linnet | *éinín bun na punainne* |
|    linnet | *gleoiseach* |
| loon | *lóma* |
| magpie | *snag breac, cabaire, míogadán* |
| mallard | *lacha bhreac, lacha riabhach* |
| Manx shearwater | *púicín gaoithe, chánóg dhubh* |
| moorhen | *cearc uisce* |
| nightingale | *smólach an bhéal bhinn* |
| owl | *mulchán, ollchaochán, cailleach oíche* |
|    barn owl | *mulchán cinn-cait* |
|    horned owl | *mulchán adharcach* |
|    screech owl | *scréachán reilige* |
|    snowy owl | *mulchán bán-geal* |
|    tawny owl | *mulchán donn, bodach oíche* |
| oystercatcher | *riabhán, giolla Bhríde* |
| partridge | *paitrisc, cearc ghearr* |
| petrel | *guardal, guairdeall, briochtóg na mara* |
|    fulmar petrel | *chánóg liath* |
|    storm petrel | *ceann biorach na stoirme, gearr úisc, gearr róide, Peadairín* (Little Peter) |
| pheasant | *coileach feá* |
|    a nide of pheasant | *ealta coileach feá* |
| pigeon, blue rock | *an colúr gorm carraige* |

| | |
|---|---|
| fantail pigeon | *colúr gabhlach* |
| plover, golden | *feadóg sléibhe* |
| puffin | *cánóg* |
|    Puffin Island, Co. Kerry | *Oileán na gCánóg* |
| quail | *gearra ghoirt, gearr naosc* |
| razorbill | *crosán, crosachán* |
| redshank | *cos deargán, faoilean cos dearg, circín trá, gabhlán mara* |
| redstart | *ceann dearg* |
| robin red breast | *spideog, spideog Mhuire* |
| sandlark | *gobadán, ceaircín trá* |
| sandmartin or    bank swallow | *gabhlán gainimhe* |
| sandpiper | *gobadán, curcach, currachóg* |
| sandtripper | *ladhrán trá* (Aran) |
| skua, great | *Tomáisín chac na bhFaoileán* (Little Tommy Gullshit), *meirleach mara* |
| snipe | *naoscach* |
| sparrow | *gealbhán* (pronounced *gealún* by author) |
|    haggard sparrow | *gealbhán sciobóil* |
|    hedge sparrow | *gealbhán tor, gob ramhar* (fat beak) |
|    house sparrow | *gealbhán tí* |
| sparrowhawk | *speirseog, spioróg spéire* |
| starling | *druid, truid* (Donegal) |
| stonechat | *caistín cloiche* |
| stork | *corr* |
|    fishing stork | *corr iasc* |
|    grey blue stork | *corr ghlas* |
| swallow | *fáinleog, áinle, áinleog* |
| swan | *eala, géis, searfán* |
| teal | *cromlacha, pislacha* |
| tern | *geabhróg, goireog* |
| thrush | *smólach* |
|    mavis thrush | *smólach cnoic* |
|    redwing thrush | *siocán* |

| | |
|---|---|
| wagtail | *glasóg, Siobhán ghlas an charn aoiligh* |
| whinchat | *gorán* |
| widgeon | *praslacha, glaslacha* |
| wren | *dreoilín, dreon éin* (taken from the words *dair éin* or *doire éan*, 'bird of the oak wood') |
| gold-crested wren | *éan a' cinn bhuí* |

# IV

## *Life on Shore*

# COASTGUARDS AND SHIPWRECK

The Coastguard Station was part of rural life along the entire coastline of Ireland. Built towards the end of the eighteenth century, the stations flourished during the nineteen hundreds and were manned by a reduced personnel until the end of the 1914 world conflict. Vitally important in the eyes of the British empire and the sea lords of the Admiralty, they were closely linked on the Iveragh coast at Waterville, Ballinskelligs, Portmagee, Valentia, Cahersiveen and Kells.

The Ballinskelligs Station situated at Reen consisted of five residential buildings in a terrace, a boathouse with a slipway and longboat, together with a private residence for the head officer, Captain John McGready. John Harms, Harry Knox and Bob Twomey lived in the married quarters. Their children attended Ballinskelligs National School (opened 1867), where they learned English, in a townland where Irish was the spoken language of the entire peasant population.

According to stories relating to the period, it is evident that Captain McGready was not popular among the people or his men. His rigid observance of the law was known to one and all. Even the most barnacled and battered piece of driftwood was to be regarded as Crown property and therefore surrendered to the Revenue Commissioners. McGready was also known to inflict penalties on men for any laxity of rules.

The ruined monastery of Saint Michael's Abbey was once a seat of learning in the thirteenth century, under the Order of Augustinian Canons, until it was despoiled during the regimes of Elizabeth and Cromwell. This lonely ruined roofless sanctuary by the sea became the first Christian burial ground in Ballinskelligs, with its Romanesque fire-blackened walls and its Gothic bell-tower, full of crude strange structural tombs, where an erring coastguard would be detailed to stand watch at the sudden whim of a strict captain.

A story was told of a young man who, having never endeared himself to Captain McGready, was ordered to stand guard within the ruins, one dark and stormy night, as a precaution against smuggling. The young coastguard standing beside a tomb during his lonely vigil observed what he thought was movement somewhere nearby. Getting down on all fours, the coastguard crawled around in a circle until, to his surprise, he saw a figure of a man in close proximity in front, standing still, whom he recognized as his Captain. Jumping forward, he thrust the barrel of his carbine between the kidneys of his superior officer, shouting, 'Don't move or you're dead.' John McGready didn't panic, saying, 'Don't shoot, Tommy. I only came to keep you company', which of course wasn't true. This was the last time a man was detailed to stand watch in the ruined Abbey.

Coastguards were mostly naval reservists, or men approaching the end of their service, trained in the Nelsonian tradition in the use of firearms, swordplay with cutlass, how to engage in hand-to-hand combat and how to repel a boarding party.

Paddy Haren's tavern was one of the licensed premises in Ballinskelligs at the time. The other was Paddy Ó Céitinn's, 'Keating's', in Dungegan. Paddy Haren was a Clare man, and a retired naval officer; hence the coastguards and the local fishermen frequented his bar. Paddy kept a plentiful supply of ship's rum, thick and dark. It was readily available in wooden casks, imported in its purest form. A thimbleful of undiluted black honey would sweep your throat free from all germs and was much sought after by men of the sea.

Old Donal McCarthy drank here also. The old man witnessed the Famine, its aftermath, the years of recovery and the shameful spectacle of faction fighting between cudgel-wielding clans. He too, among others, was expert in the use of the cudgel in self-defence. This art was the equivalent of the cut, thrust and parry of swordplay, as practised in the naval sailing fleet of the time. The faction-fighting clans called this form of self-defence *Boiscín,* or

'boskeen'. The so-called shillelagh took the
Irish shillelagh-wielders were known to have
men.

Coastguard Tommy Adams suspected that old Do.
haps an expert in the use of the shillelagh as a weapon ot
fence and therefore wished to test the old man's skill. Then ca..
the day when the old man grew tired of Adam's persistent chal-
lenging him to fight a duel with cudgels. At last, Donal accepted
the challenge. The proprietor of the tavern, Paddy Haren, was appointed the referee. The winner was to be the contestant who first
made bodily contact three times. He would receive a half bottle of
ship's rum, the loser a quart of ale. Each man was to have the approved shillelagh of equal design. A day was appointed and the
floor of the tavern cleared of furniture. The bout itself was to be
kept secret, in case the law would frown on such an activity.

Old McCarthy, divested of his jacket and homespun gansey,
rolled up his sleeves and carefully pulled his stockings over the hem
of his frieze trousers, before taking off his heavy brogues and stepping nimbly on his vamps. With Donal's scant grey locks and
beady blue eyes, he performed a short ritual dance, twirling his
shillelagh like some Zulu warrior. The coastguard explained very
sincerely to the old man that he only wanted to ascertain the truth
of whether the Irish stick-wielders were skilled in the art of fencing. McCarthy replied, '*B'fhearr dhuit ciall a bheith agat*', meaning,
'Better for you to be sensible.'

Paddy Haren who was also a swordsman, bringing the two un-
equal protagonists together, advised them to show their skill in
imitating sword play and, drawing a line on the floor, he called the
word, 'Advance!' following in raised voice, 'On guard', then the
final word, 'Go.'

Old Donal danced like a paper doll and it was soon evident that
he was under pressure from a very skilled adversary, a product of
naval training. As yet an opening for a touch had not presented itself. Old McCarthy was backed into a corner. Then it happened:
the knob of Donal's shillelagh made contact over the coastguard's
left ear. Tommy Adams winced under the sudden stinging impact,

*y* to receive two more resounding taps in quick succession, dictly in line over the left ear.

Paddy Haren stepped in, declaring the contest over. Adams shook the old man's hand, who remarked, '*Ná dúirt mé leat ciall a bheith agat*', meaning, 'I told you have sense.' Three lumps like thrush's eggs began to grow over Tommy's ear, to which he applied cold water. This convinced him that cudgel fighting and fencing derived from the same art. The above account I heard from my cousin, old John Fitzgerald of Horse Island.

The coastguard's long boat was thirty-five feet overall by seven feet beam, propelled by oar and sail, built to endure and be seaworthy in severe conditions. The boat and gear were always tested during a regular monthly drill. During the last century of sail, many fine ships were abandoned at sea, several for unknown reasons, with full cargoes and sound rigging. Ships abandoned in the Atlantic drifted on to the south-west coast of Ireland; several foundering on rock-bound inlets of South Kerry.

One such ship was a four-masted barque, the *Nielsen Hauge*. With full rig, it was seen to sail slowly from the west into the outer reaches of St Finan's Bay. On the second day the wind dropped, leaving the ship becalmed, only to drift aimlessly, '*as idle as a painted ship upon a painted ocean*'. It was not unusual to see a ship becalmed, especially when having plenty of sea room. Towards the evening of the third day, a wind came up from a south-westerly direction, filling the idle sails of the becalmed vessel. Suddenly the sails billowed with a strengthening breeze, driving the vessel on an erratic course towards the rock-bound Finan's Bay. People on the shore, becoming suspicious, prompted local fishermen to launch a boat. The fishermen rowed within hailing distance of the ship but no life was observed on deck. The westerly wind had grown to gale force, making it urgent that the fishermen return to shore. By this time the ship had drifted towards the high craggy cliffs of 'Tooreen', *Túairín*.

The people of St Finan's Glen who watched from the cliff-side saw the stately barque drift towards her last resting place, the kelp floor of *Cuas an Túairín*, in ten fathoms of clear Atlantic water.

How often did she bring joy to a sailor's heart, running down her easterlies under full canvas, or bounding across the line with a bone in her teeth? It was a sad sight surely, without a master's confident, gentle touch on her helm. The hand to steer her safely through the perils of the mighty ocean had now forsaken her. *Bád gan stiúr nó cú gan eireaball*, meaning 'a ship without a rudder, or a hound without a tail'. No lively crew to trim her down or man the capstan. She was rocking and rolling, drifting helplessly, like a dead seabird, caught in the froth of an ocean current. A westerly, long, rolling swell developed, which increased with a flood tide.

Inch by inch, the once stately barque drifted, until at last the top rail of the *Nielsen Hauge* seemed to caress the toothed crag, her cross trees now and then touching the cliff-face. A long rolling swell, carrying a white curl on its lip, caught her amidships, causing violent contact with the more shallow ledges. With each rise and fall, a grinding, creaking, sickening sound of wood cracking developed. The crashing of spars, the tearing of shrouds, as she listed, showing a gaping tear below and above her water line, refusing to founder, because of her cargo of pine. She continued to break up, spewing her great cargo, until the waters of the cove were covered with planks of all dimensions, great beams, trebles and scantlings. The tip of the main mast remained visible for some days. A sad reminder of how a ship can die.

As shades of evening darkened, the local folk tried to salvage some of the valuable planks by working constantly into the night, knowing that on the morrow, their efforts would be restricted by servants of the Crown. It was, at most, a desperately hazardous task. Men could be seen standing on dangerous rock shelves with casting hooks, gaffs, and ropes, using any method to salvage a plank, risking their lives time and again, enveloped in the obscurity of a dashing drenching murky sea spray. Willing hands worked unceasingly, pulling on ropes attached to planks. They hid the wreckage among furze and rocks on the nearby hillside, away from the prying eyes of John McGready, who arrived on the scene the next day, when news of the shipwreck had reached him at Rinn Coastguard Station. He immediately placed the salvage operation under the watchful eyes of his men, armed with carbines, making it clear to the natives that anyone found guilty of concealing or taking planks for their own use would be prosecuted and suffer severe penalties. A local man called Murphy was appointed to keep record of the amount each person had salvaged. They would receive only a pittance for their labours.

The coastguards kept weary vigil during the wet foggy nights, which very much hampered the strict surveillance they were to observe. Often what was salvaged by day seemed to mysteriously disappear under cover of darkness. My father, helped by his cousins, the Fentons of Coom, together with other neighbours, concealed a goodly amount of the splendid pitch pine under the deep heather and bracken of the hillside. The work required Herculean effort on their part: such was the desire of the people to outwit the servants of the Crown!

To many people the windfall of the *Nielsen Hauge* became a godsend. The timber wrested from the sea and from the Realm, however illicit it might seem, helped to repair the roofs of the old thatched hovels of that period.

Some years previous another fine ship called the *Menthaur*, laden with a cargo of dried fruit from Greece, mostly raisins, packed in wooden boxes, was seen by the Coastguards, drifting dangerously close to the reef, called in Irish, *Dingeacha na Scairbhe*, 'the Scarrif Island Wedges'. The reef resembles a set of large stone wedges, as if driven in by some giant hand. On perceiving the plight of the hitherto unknown vessel, John McGready and his 'Jolly Tars' wasted no time. Launching the long boat, they were soon seen pulling lustily across the bay, each man swinging to his oar with muscular precision, the Captain himself at the tiller exhorting his crew to put their backs into it, 'with a heave ho, my hearties'. On reaching the *Menthaur* and having hailed her, they decided to put a crew on board, finding no sign of human life, except a cat so scrawny and pitiful, perhaps using the last hours of its ninth life!

To John McGready and his crew the ship presented a valuable boon in prize money. Therefore, they set about sailing the ship across the bay. Helped by a southerly breeze, under the shelter of Horse Island, Captain John brought the vessel into safe anchorage in seven fathoms of water. It seemed so simple an operation to a trained crew, the task of dropping anchor, but some unknown fate decided otherwise. As the heavy chain started its run, a tangled loop of cable formed a knot, unyielding to any frantic effort of John McGready or his men. The hawse port remained totally obstructed, preventing the anchor from reaching the floor of the harbour. The *Menthaur* drifted astern, helped to what seemed her inescapable doom, by the same southerly breeze that seemed so favourable only moments before. In very short time the ship grounded between the teeth of *Rinn Dubh* and *Boilg Anders*, as the tide ebbed the *Menthaur* lay on her beam ends across the reef, spiked to her last resting-place, thus depriving the coastguards of prize money.

The Revenue Commissioners took the cargo and all things moveable, leaving only the hull, which was covered with copper sheeting. The local peasantry, working under the cover of darkness, removed some of the valuable sheeting and sold it to scrap dealers which in turn infuriated Captain McGready who placed an immediate armed guard on the wreck when the tide was out. Despite his strict administration of the law, little pieces of the stranded hull kept on disappearing until large holes appeared and the copper was no longer visible. Helped by a winter storm, the hull of the *Menthaur* became a total wreck, in which the authorities held no further interest.

Some years prior to 1847, another crewless ship was driven ashore at a place called *Bun na Féithe*, 'bottom of the marsh', on Inny Strand. I heard local historians refer to it by its cargo as *Long an ghráinne bhuí*. The vessel carried in its hold a cargo of Indian corn from the Americas. The authorities were unable to remove the entire cargo, owing to the short time available to them, before the hull became completely engulfed by the bed of quicksand on which she had landed.

Some years later, when grim famine stalked the land, South Iveragh was no exception. A large peasant population struggled to survive starvation; hoards of emaciated people roamed the roads of Munster suffering the gnawing pains of hunger.

People were drawn to the foreshore, the strands and the beaches; a crude net, a little boat or even a fishing line would make the difference between survival and an early grave. Because of the edible shellfish, groups were seen to forage among the rock pools as the tide receded, even edible seaweeds were boiled and eaten, anything to allay and slake the terrible hunger. One day some local fishermen in the course of conversation mentioned how welcome a shipload of Indian corn would be, like *Long an ghráinne bhuí* that lay beneath the sand at *Bun na Féithe*, with most of its precious cargo still in its hold.

Someone suggested that a portion of the cargo might still be free from dampness. In this case, hunger became the mother of urgency. Without further ado, a group of local men armed with long iron rods converged on the sand at *Bun na Féithe*. They began probing the sand in the place where the vessel was supposed to lie.

A number of days elapsed before finding the wreck under six feet of sand. She was lying on her beam-ends, very near the high-water mark of a spring tide. This was favourable for the excavation of sand when the moon was on the wane with slack tides. A throng of near starving people commenced to shovel away the sand. The prospect of finding food uppermost in their minds, they worked feverishly, keeping the area clear of water, digging canals and bailing with buckets.

At last, to the great excitement of the workers, the bulging planks of a wooden ship became exposed. It was then the local tradesmen took over; the blacksmith, the cooper and carpenter, using sharp tools cut a large hole into the hull of *Long an ghráinne bhuí*. A medical man gave advice about gas or contaminated grain. A large cheer went up when it was discovered that a goodly portion of the grain was still dry and free from damp. If boiled for gruel, it was found fit to eat; a people who were hungry were not choosy about the menu.

The coastguard barracks are now firmly entrenched in the past. Only roofless ruins to remind us, standing as visible evidence of an imperial colonization. *Nielsen Hauge,* the *Menthaur, Long an ghráinne bhuí* and many others become ghost ships of the past that keep on sailing, dipping and appearing on the horizon of my memory, helped by little wavelets from the storytellers of my youth.

# FLOATING MINES

Whatever knowledge I have in regard to floating mines comes from the fact of having examined the interior of a device, which the expert rendered harmless. He kindly explained to me its mechanics and how the explosion was triggered. I do not wish to pontificate or set myself up, other than to relate as best I can, of my experience as a fisherman and the happenings in my own locality with regard to floating mines.

Floating explosives at sea were much more in evidence during the last war, than that of 1914. The floating mine became a lethal scientific instrument of death and destruction. Many and various were the designs created by the armament engineers of the warring nations, electronic science playing a more significant part in the latter years. Cunning devices such as the magnetic and later the acoustic mine were invented, manufactured and used with deadly accuracy. The magnetic device was sown in the narrow shipping lanes leading to harbours, and in the more important ports. Like mines of the magnetic device, the acoustic mine could be sown from the air in narrow estuaries. The magnetic device was triggered by proximity of the ship's hull, while the acoustic mine was triggered by the throbbing sound of an internal combustion engine or the whirring of an electric turbine.

The most common device was cone-shaped, like a child's spinning top or a giant hen egg. Some mines were five feet in height, weighed five hundred pounds, and had a diameter of fifty inches. The explosive substance, which looked like a type of grey butter, was contained in a separate cylinder of steel, within the interior of the mine and would weigh at least two hundred pounds. Heavy spiral coil steel springs were compressed with nuts and bolts on the explosive chamber to increase its power. The minor detonators, which protruded through the outer shell, called the horns of the mine, were each, in turn, wired to the main detonator and connected to a watertight system of electric spark.

I had occasion to witness a large mine being rendered harmless by an army officer who was qualified to deal with such an emergency. I remember while on our way to the fishing grounds, on the southern approach to Ballinskelligs Bay, we were about to cast our train of mackerel nets, when I was ordered by our captain, who was on the forepart of the boat, on the lookout for signs of mackerel schools, to change course because of some large, partly submerged object directly in front of our line of passage. It was our first sighting of a large mine of German – as we discovered at a later date – manufacture. It stood upright in the water, exactly like a spinning top, and kept continually rocking like a child's cradle. Even in the gentle swell it rocked and half spun, bobbing its horned head as if to mock us. A large lifting ring eyebolt topped its umbrella-like pot. It bristled with horns, each at least twelve inches in length.

As night was falling, we waited in the vicinity of the unwelcome infernal intruder, which had strayed and entered our peaceful waters, until we showed its position to Jim Fitzgerald's boat, which was travelling in our direction. Having decided to keep well windward of the troublesome wayfarer, we entered our bay by a different route. We expected to find the mine washed ashore onto one of the local beaches sometime the next day. The wind blew favourably for days on end. Every fisherman and even the Corvette scoured the area to no avail. The local coast watchers and police began to think it was a hoax and that we had invented a tall one. As time went by, we fishermen often discussed among ourselves, the disappearance of the mine and came to the conclusion it had to drift ashore locally.

Several weeks passed before the mysterious mine made local

news once more. Old men and younger women, the postman, the sergeant of the Garda, the parish priest and his housekeeper, the local butcher, the shopkeeper and the blacksmith who crowned it all with; 'Did you hear the latest? Wasn't he lucky! One belt of the sledge and his ghost would go to heaven so quickly he'd stretch St Peter in the door.'

The elusive mine went ashore at high tide on the tip of Bolus Head, where it sat perched on top of a flat rock in a precarious position, with the cliff-face towering above. It was not known for wreckage to be found in this most exposed headland, and how it managed to float into place without exploding baffled the experts. It seems that a local farmer had been searching for a missing sheep, and happening to notice the strange object, he climbed down the cliff-face to investigate. Having inspected the mine, he decided it wasn't a very useful contraption, except for the iron horns of course. Oh, the very thing, they'd make excellent bolts to replace the worn ones on his wooden-frame farm harrow. If only he had a hammer or a sledge. With the help of a piece of rock he managed to bend one bolt a little sideways but failed to dislodge it. He decided to call on his neighbour, Seamus Fada, for the loan of a heavy hammer, some other tools and perhaps a word of advice as well. Seamus Fada was known by one and all to be one of the most knowledgeable men in the locality. You could ask him any question from astronomy to a cure for smelly feet. As for guns and powder and bombs, wasn't he with the Munsters at Mons. Seamus declined point blank to loan his neighbour the hammer but decided instead to accompany him to the scene where the horned monster sat sedately on the only flat rock to be found from there to *Oileán na bhFaoileán*, 'the island of gulls'. Seamus Fada surveyed the mine and recognized immediately the danger of the situation.

'Somebody must have saved you from a sudden death, Seán', he said. 'If you hit the tip of the bolt that you bent sideways, you'd have no need for the heavy hammer, you'd be judged, damned or sainted by now. I don't like the bristling hairpins on that *biorránach's* head. Come let's go and report the matter to the coast watchers.'

Some hours later an army officer inspected the uninvited blow-in, which had taken up residence and was sitting smugly like a horned toad on the tip of Bolus headland. The army officer ordered the area leading to the cliff to be sealed off from the general public, until the mine was examined in more detail. The usual type of mine was of British manufacture but this one was made in Germany.

Several days elapsed before the experts decided that, owing to being tampered with by Seán, the damaged detonator was on a very delicate hair trigger and would warrant no rough handling. When all was ready, the army laid a wire connected to an explosive charge over the brow of the cliff, which they attached to the mine. Before they pressed the plunger they had ordered the natives to open all doors and windows. A terrible explosion rocked the evening air leaving a yellow white scar on the cliff-face that was visible for many a day.

Some mines broke loose from their moorings. One such mine drifted into our bay, trailing its mooring until finally getting held up on rough ground inshore. A naval corvette destroyed it by gunfire. Some smaller mines were tied in pairs with a spacing wire of many fathoms between them. The bow of the ship would connect with the spacing wire thereby causing a double explosion.

Irish mackerel fishermen were fearful of floating mines, not so much of colliding with them in the hours of darkness but of coming into close contact when entangled in their nets. This usually meant cutting away valuable fishing gear and steering clear of any intimate relations with the unwelcome toad. One calm night while hauling mackerel nets near the Skellig Rock, a large mine appeared very close to the side of the mackerel-fishing trawl. A member of the crew delicately manoeuvred the mine clear of the boat's stern with the help of a long wooden handle of a boat hook, while another fisherman kept a light trained on it.

The rock-bound shore of the Iveragh peninsula served as protection against accident by helping to trigger mines that bumped against the cliff-face. It was not unusual to hear the rumble of a loud explosion disturb the peaceful air of the locality, followed by screaming of gulls on the headlands or the sudden stampeding of cattle. On one such occasion, a horse with a loaded creel of peat took fright on a local bogland, ending up in a capsized and wrecked position. The aggrieved farmer, knowing there would never be any form of redress or compensation from the warring empire builders, could only find consolation in consigning them all to hell.

# BALLINSKELLIGS CABLE STATION

The first submarine cable was laid from the United States to Ballinskelligs in 1875. The cable was called the D.U.S., an abbreviation for Direct Union States. The station buildings were constructed by a London-based company in about the year 1865. English and Scottish contractors were employed. The buildings were of mass concrete construction and consisted of the main offices, a clock tower and modern living quarters, in an enclosed compound comprising three or four acres. Gardens were attached to each dwelling. The whole area was enclosed by a well-built wall. Spring-water was supplied by gravity flow from the base of a hill, about a mile distant. There were septic tanks and a complete sewer system for modern bathrooms, and also plumbing providing hot and cold water. The lighting was provided by a carbide gas plant built on the premises. A wooden church with bell and tower was also built on the compound.

The station had its own fire-fighting equipment, with engine house and pressure pumps to pump water from the sea in case of fire. This equipment was installed by a company called 'Merry-weather' of London. There were stables with two horses and a covered wagon with a full-time stableman, a cartage man, a battery man and a man to attend to the lighting system, thereby giving full-time employment to four local people. A cook with four domestic servants was in charge of the mess and kitchens, providing meals for the staff and those operators who lived in the unmarried quarters. The housekeeper was Margaret Shea from Kenneigh near Waterville, and the cook was Mary O'Sullivan from Boolakeel. Michael Sugrue of Dungeagan was the local butcher who supplied the fresh mutton and other meats. The bulk of their vegetables were grown locally.

Their recreation consisted of an up-to-date billiards room and lawns for their tennis club. With their families in residence, the entire group would average eighty to a hundred persons. The place was kept very neat with many gardens, flowerbeds and shrubs. A boathouse on the beach provided shelter for sailing yachts and fishing equipment. The superintendent's residence was in another location apart from the station. It was a modern three-storied English building like that provided for a country squire, with gateways and a driveway. I remember some names of the officials and staff.

Superintendents: Mr Topping; Mr Blenheim; Mr Lloyd. Head Operators: Mr Main (Falkirk); Mr Armstrong (English Midlands); Mr Waterstone; Mr Cobley; Mr Stone; Mr Seekins; Mr Westbrook; Mr Faircloud; Mr McMichael; Mr Ratton. Censors: Mr Spencer; Mr Nash; Mr Higgs; Mr Watson; Mr Moore; Mr Harty; Mr Cornwall; Mr Drum; Mr Sullivan; Mr Keating; Mr Golden; Mr Thompson – resident carpenter; Mr Foll; Mr Broderick; Mr Rickard; Mr W. Goggin (Ballinskelligs) – battery attendant, later transferred to Fanning Island in the Pacific Ocean, where the company maintained another cable station. Mr Sugrue, operator, was a native of Valentia Island. Mr O'Connell and Mr Jerome Sullivan were natives of the locality. Mr O'Connell's son later became the first clerk of Dáil Éireann.

The earliest repair ship involved in cable laying, that I can remember, was a ship called the *Buccaneer*. I heard my father say that a pilot from Valentia named McCrohan would come over land to Ballinskelligs, where a local crew awaited him at the old fishing pier to meet the ship as she rounded into the mouth of Ballinskelligs Bay. My father, being one of the crew, told me how the pilot would sit in the stern and steer them towards the ship and he would chant a little rhyme in rhythm with each oar stroke: *Pull boys pull, there's smoke off the Bull.* Meaning of course that he, the pilot, saw the black smoke from her funnels appearing near the Bull Rock. The *Great Eastern* was the ship that laid the cable through the deepest part of the Atlantic, and only came to the mouth of the bay, where the shore end leading to Ballinskelligs beach was connected to the Atlantic through a smaller diameter cable. I remember seeing a ship called the *Colonia* and a smaller inshore repair ship, *Lady of the Isles.* The *Lord Kelvin* was a great four thousand tonner. Other ships of one thousand tons were the *John W. MacCay*, the *George Ward* and the *Marie Louise MacCay.* Those latter-named ships were all used for coastal repair.

A story is told, about the day when the first shore end was brought onto the beach in the spring of 1875. The big ship manoeuvred as close to the beach as possible, taking advantage of the high water peak of a spring tide. The cumbersome, heavy cable was coiled onto flat, raft-like boats, which would float into shallow water. Large numbers of peasantry were assembled on the beach, watching the wonder of a transatlantic cable being brought ashore. The foreman in charge of the operation had harnessed two local draught horses to a rope attached to the end of the cable. All went well, until strain was applied to the rope and, helped by a gentle swell, the nearest float to the shore overturned, spilling the coiled cable into six feet of water. At this stage, the horses proved very ineffective because of soft sand. The foreman, being a very astute person, stumbled on another bright idea.

Seeing the potent pulling power of the large crowd, he proceeded to bargain with them. Every able-bodied man who would help pull the cable ashore was to be paid two shillings and six pence. He would need forty men, and as an incentive the first man who would lay hands on the cable was to be given a half sovereign in gold. No sooner said than done. The hired men rushed headlong into the broken wave where the cable lay.

One man outstripped them all, with a mighty leap and dived into the sea. Grasping the end, he tore it loose from the coil and helped by the rest of the hired team pulled the cable up the sandy beach in front of the cable buildings. True to his word, the foreman paid each person two and six pence, and calling for the man who merited the gold coin, asked for his name and address. The man in question was Denis O'Leary from Ballinskelligs. On presenting him with the coin and holding O'Leary's arm aloft in a gesture of victory, the foreman announced that from hence forward the cable would be called 'Cable O'Leary'. The name stuck – not on the cable, but on Denis, who was known as 'the Cable' from then on. The next generation inherited the name and to this day their progeny are referred to as the 'Cable O'Learys'. The family was already famous, being the last to fight the rack-rent bailiffs, the sheriff and the redcoats with pitchforks during their eviction in 1864. I saw pictures of the eviction taken by a photographer, one Mr Cuthbert, who was connected with the construction of the cable company. The pictures, in sepia tones on a glossy tin plate, showed the peasantry of the time in their wretched clothing, barefoot people wearing long unkempt hair. Those noble but crestfallen people were my ancestors.

The station flourished for more than half a century. Many tales were told by old people, who could not understand a word of the clipped English accent and whose means of communication was 'the sweet and kindly' Irish. One of the cable superintendents was a Mr Topping, he kept a huge St Bernard. A breed of dog which is usually very docile, this specimen had a ferocious bark and a mean-looking face. In fact, the local people lived in fear of the animal, which was known to the Irish-speaking community as *gadhar mhór Topping*, or 'Topping's big dog'.

At that time we had a change of clergymen, a new curate and Parish Priest both at the same time. The curate was a very gentle priest, always speaking about the good influence of the Holy Spirit in our lives. The P.P. by contrast was very gruff and spoke in a booming, threatening voice. One day when the new curate visited our school he asked the children how they liked their new pastors. The teacher wished that the ground would swallow him on hearing one little fellow tell the astonished curate, he had heard his father say that one was like the Holy Ghost and the other had a bark like Topping's dog.

Another old lady, who had but few words of English, told me how she was collecting carrageen moss among the rocks, on the shore near the cable station when she heard a conversation in English between two men. One was the captain of a small steamboat, whose anchor got badly fouled on the newly laid cable close to the shore. The crew of the ship were making frantic efforts to release the anchor, while officials of the cable company stood on the shore. Speaking on a loudhailer, they remonstrated with the captain of the ship, shouting: 'Go away and don't smash our cable!' To which the captain would shout back: 'F*** you and your bloody cable.' The old woman told me that she asked her sailor brother, what was the meaning of this was. To which he replied that it was a word they used whenever they had difficulty with hauling an anchor. She asked me if this was the real meaning of the word concerned and I said that I supposed her brother had given her the correct information.

When the 1914 war broke out, the British government took precautions in protecting the station, with an impenetrable barrier of barbed wire. The barrier was ten feet across, with wooden oak stakes eight feet high, driven deeply into the ground. The wire was coiled in spirals, in a fashion that made it impossible for a human to crawl through, without cutting himself every inch of the way. The entire compound was surrounded on all sides, guarded day and night by a platoon of twenty-one men and officers who lived in wooden quarters built within the area. Three sentry boxes were occupied full-time, one guarding the beach and two on the approaching roads.

The first platoon – the infamous Scottish Borders – wore kilts, and then there were the Sherwood Foresters, who crawled up Sackville Street in 1916 to quell the Irish Rebels. Later on I saw veterans of the Munster Fusiliers, who were given a stint of a couple of months in Ireland, before returning to the trenches. I saw them march eleven dusty miles from the railhead in Cahersiveen to Ballinskelligs, each wearing full pack and rifle; old hardened war dogs, who had served the empire well, sometimes dubbed by the British Tommies, 'the Dirty Shirts'. This very regiment were the men who covered themselves with glory by breaking the German line with fixed bayonets and saving the guns at the Battle of Mons. The old ballad sung in their praise:

*Who saved the guns that day at Mons, the Munster Fusileers!*

Some very beautiful English girls lived in the cable station. I remember some of their names like Florrie Westbrook, Inez Cornwall, Kathleen McMichael, Beatty Stone and several Armstrong girls, one maiden more beautiful than the other. Natalie Lloyd, the superintendent's daughter, and of course the Main girls, were beautiful and distinctive looking, not forgetting the spouses of the officials, who were all fine specimens of womanhood.

The tennis club took part in tournaments between Waterville and Valentia cable stations. A nice wooden Protestant church was built on the grounds. It was used by the community for Sunday school and for regular service, held by the Reverend Parson Fahy who resided in Waterville and travelled to Ballinskelligs by pony and trap. Some Irish operators were discharged from service on suspicion that their families were sympathetic towards Sinn Féin during the 1916 Rising. The cable community kept very much aloof from the local peasantry and preferred not to mix, sometimes organizing their own private entertainment such as garden parties and private dances.

During the war years the cable office was eternally busy working in shifts, night and day, in communication with the United States and the Colonies. All messages were scrutinized by official censors placed on the station. The company, owned by American and British millionaires MacCay and Bennett, was terminated in 1918. The cables were connected to Penzance and to the British and French network. Some operators retained their jobs, being transferred to Penzance, some to Key West, Miami, and others to the United States and London. Afterwards, the buildings were used for summer Irish Language courses, and later were totally demolished.

I worked for the commercial cable company of Waterville doing interior decoration. This gave me a certain knowledge regarding the interior of a transatlantic operating station. There were large, wet battery rooms, heated rooms, keeping certain instruments at proper temperature, dark rooms with cable-testing equipment, rooms showing large charts of the Atlantic seabed. With the advent of Teletype, television and telex, computers, the Internet, e-mail, etc., these new technologies make those instruments look like pieces from the Stone Age. One computer can now operate and control an entire floor, where hitherto twenty operators were employed to take and send signals of communication. In another decade of centuries, I have no doubt, man will have discovered telepathy and how to harness the sub-conscious mind. Then one might ask the question, 'Whither go'est thou, Homo sapiens?'

I have in my possession a dated and brassbound section of the transatlantic submarine cable, which was laid into Ballinskelligs Bay in 1875 and 1896; also transmitting form No. 3 of the Direct United States Cable Co. Ltd, showing a copy of a message received at Ballinskelligs Cable Station on the 3rd September 1894; the receiving clerk was Mr Cobley. There is also a copy of a code message from New York to Paris, dated 14th February 1923, and specimen recorder slips of tape, showing direct, main-cable duplex signals.

It is said that Cable Company personnel generally ignored the local peasantry, whom they considered too low a class with which to fraternise. This is not surprising because the surrounding area at that period was designated a Congested Districts area, having no industries, a large population, bad housing and small holdings of land carrying high rent and rates. Many people lived very close to the poverty line. The Realm was not interested in the welfare of the peasantry of the locality, and this state of administration only led to the inevitable Rebellion of 1916.

A member of the Armstrong family, Herbert, who was born in Ballinskelligs and died in Vernon, British Columbia, Canada, presented the above items to me. His father John Garnet Armstrong, an Englishman born in Carlisle, Cumbria, beside the Scottish border, was a Catholic. John married Margaret Harty, a member of a well-respected local farming family. He died at the early age of forty-nine, leaving a large family of eleven.

I am pleased to say that John Armstrong's attitude towards the local people was on the most friendly of terms. He wrote numerous letters to government departments, and attended meetings on behalf of the rights of the needy. Another very popular English man was Mr Westbrook, who died in his native England, living to the fine old age of one hundred and one years.

The Seekins family were also well-respected. William George Seekins died in Miami at age eighty-five. He was born in London and began working as a boy at the Cable Station in Ballinskelligs under the tuition of his father. He was later transferred to the station in Newfoundland, Halifax, where he received from England the message that the *Titanic* had sunk, on 15 April 1912, with a loss of 1517 lives. He was the first to relay the fatal message to New York and the New World. He was later transferred from Halifax, Nova Scotia, to Miami Beach Station, where he served as superintendent for twenty-five years.

Not all the clerks at the Cable Station were competent to man the receiving signals on tape. Mr Colby was one of the best, but Mortimer O'Connell was the best operator for speed and accuracy. There were no typewriters in those days and the superintendent always gave O'Connell the task of writing all official letters to the Headquarters of the Cable Company in London.

Herbert Armstrong states in a letter from Vernon, June 1976, speaking in praise of O'Connell: 'In all my life I have never seen such beautiful handwriting.' John Garnet Armstrong was one of the first technicians of his time; along with taking part in transmitting and receiving messages, he was also the only man on the staff at Ballinskelligs who could fix the various instruments in those days of comparatively primitive machines. Trouble from magnetic and electrical interference, called induction, caused distorted cable signals that in turn reduced the efficient working of the entire system. A number of experiments were carried out by John Armstrong, and when applied, they greatly increased the quality of the cable signal to Ballinskelligs. John Armstrong's idea became standard practice on all Atlantic cables and in the course of time was improved upon. His theory was that every electric signal, whether phone or telegraph, creates a magnetic field, and any conductor picks up this and causes interference.

My dear friend Herbert Armstrong worked in the Valentia Cable Station for several years, until shortly after the Easter Rising of 1916. Valentia was originally the Anglo-American Cable Company but was gobbled up by the giant American company, the Western Union Telegraph Company. There were five cables going out from Valentia and six from Waterville and Ballinskelligs. A few days after the Easter Rebellion in 1916, the British government sent several censors to each cable station in Ireland. To quote my friend, every day for the whole twenty-four hours one of the censors was stationed at our side checking every word transmitted over the cables, all through World War One. They did not trust Irishmen working in cable stations in Ireland. The outside world knew nothing about the Rising until it was completely crushed and all the leaders executed. Some Irish operators tried to get a message through to the Irish in New York, but the censor was alert and clamped down on the transmission switch. This created quite a scare in British quarters, with the result that all the young Irishmen were transferred to different cable stations outside of Ireland, out of harm's way.

Those pioneers of cable communication were giants in their own right. Prior to the submarine cable, sailing ships took many weeks to bring mail messages across the Atlantic. The cable station cut the message time to minutes.

We have many unsung heroes, but a tribute to the cable men of the south coast of Ireland, Ballinskelligs, Waterville and Valentia! Your memory must never fail.

# BEACHCOMBERS

Was it because I had read Defoe's *Robinson Crusoe*, Ballantyne's *Coral Island* or Stevenson's *Treasure Island* that I wished to walk alone on a stretch of clean sandy beach, especially in the full of the moon? On a night such as this when the waves, breaking and trooping shoreward, have turned to a brilliant silver and when the sand and the sea take on a polished reflection, giving an added exhilaration to the expectations of the beachcomber, the thrill of finding a great spar of wood or a cask washed ashore is linked with the beauty of the night. Beachcombing can become habitual and also exciting. It held a sense of allurement for me.

A variety of flotsam, helped by ocean currents, drifted onto the south Kerry beaches during the World Wars. Wreckage was the result of the dreadful torpedo and various other devices of destruction. All kinds of valuable planks and broken wood came ashore. Ships' life-rafts and abandoned lifeboats, casks of petroleum and kerosene, large iron barrels of a liquid called acetone, lubricating oil and great wooden casks of yellow palm-oil butter. Every household had a plentiful supply of palm-oil. The casks weighed half a ton. Many casks were smashed on the rocks and great lumps of the solidified oil remained on the seashore, there for the taking. The oil had many uses. It was used for chapped hands, stiff joints, infected cuts, waterproofing heavy, hobnailed, leather boots and even for axle grease on farm carts. Bales of raw rubber and cotton were commonplace. Packs of rubber contraceptive devices of American manufacture also became victim to the torpedo blast. The caves and beaches were strewn with what present day society call condoms. I heard one old man ask his son, 'What kind of damn things are these?'

All wreckage was to be surrendered to the Revenue Commissioners under the Merchant Shipping Act of 1800. This law was never observed by the beachcombers, if at all possible. In the gospel of the beachcomber, the great 'Caesar' was not to be rendered to, or become a beneficiary. The Royal Irish Constabulary kept a very watchful eye on such illegal activity. Nevertheless, some of the rank and file constables proved unfaithful to His Majesty by helping the natives move barrels to a secret rendezvous, where a buyer would pick them up. All was done in strict secrecy for a deserving share of the loot. The constables wore civilian garb for these nocturnal deceptions. The natives used a code of names, such as 'Washtub' when referring to the wreckage of casks washed up on the shore. Planks were 'sticks', iron casks were 'drums' and poles were 'bullets'. Some casks of rum and whiskey were washed ashore. Most dangerous of all were the large floating mines, bedecked with horned, sensitive detonators.

Two neighbours of mine, Jamesie Stock and Paddy Tom, were beachcombers of a different kind. They were perpetually on the prowl, dawn to dusk or midnight – whenever wind or tides favoured them. They could smell a barnacled object that had floated ashore in the darkness of night. They had found, salvaged and sold what other folk would leave behind. Jamesie Stock lived alone in a cottage overlooking the beach and, like a cormorant on a rock, not even a bottle floated ashore but Jamesie's watchful eye floated beside it. Paddy Tom lived with his mother Sheila. Only a green field separated both dwellings. Sheila was a very austere woman. Her husband Thomas had flown the coop with a younger pullet many years earlier. Both disappeared into the oblivion of America, leaving Sheila to bring up her baby Paddy, who was now showing a few extra wrinkles above the eyebrows, still unmarried, but still Mom's kinky-headed little boy.

One night while Jamesie and Paddy were having one last prowl on the beach before departing for their separate homes, Jamesie observed what seemed to be a cask bobbing among the breakers, coming nearer the shore until they could see it more clearly. Wading into the sea, they rolled it onto the hard sand until they were well beyond high-water mark. On examining the wooden cask with lighted matches, they concluded from the markings that it contained some kind of alcohol. 'Where do we put it?' asked Jamesie. 'We can't take it home,' said Paddy. 'My mother would mess up everything.' 'I know where we'll hide it', said Jamesie, 'in *Poll a' Chait.*' 'The entrance to that place is overgrown for years and besides, the cave is full of wild cats', countered Paddy. 'The last wild cat I heard tell of must be as old as the hag of Beara', said Jamesie. 'I'll bring the wheelbarrow', replied Paddy. 'It will take some *mulliking* to bring it up the *cumar* (ravine).' 'That's a desperate cross place,' said Jamesie. 'Bring the auger and the brass tap. Don't forget the hurricane lantern. It will be dark in *Poll a' Chait.*'

Jamesie stood guard until Paddy arrived with the barrow. They both lifted the cask and set it in a reclining position on the small vehicle. *Poll a' Chait* was about two hundred yards above high-water mark. The way leading up to the little cave, hidden in the ravine, was the bed of a rivulet, which ran dry in hot summers. It was strewn with rough stones and boulders. During the ages the little mountain stream had gouged out a fissure with clay walls to a depth of twenty feet in some parts. The mouth of the cave was difficult to find as it was entirely obscured with wild Sally brambles, furze, briars and ferns.

After much puffing and panting, swaying and stumbling in the dim half-light, the undaunted pair eventually arrived at the entrance of *Poll a' Chait.* Jamesie decided they must rest awhile before entering the cave. Leaving the barrow outside, it was with some trepidation that the anxious beachcombers lit the hurricane lamp and crawled into the cave. The interior was spacious and dry, with a rocky ceiling. The floor was on a higher level than the bed of the ravine, and reaching back some distance. The light revealed a rusty skillet pot. The staves and hoops of a collapsed cask were evidence of past occupation.

Just as Paddy bent down to examine the old skillet, a large otter slithered by, making for the exit. Paddy jumped with fright saying, 'I thought it was a wild cat.' 'Come let us get the cask inside,' said Jamesie, 'it is getting late.' There was just enough space to ease the cask through the doorway. They brought some large stones from the rear of the cave, forming an improvised platform on which they set the barrel. Producing the auger, Jamesie chose the exact position on the cask, where he instantly bored and inserted the brass tap with a few deft blows from a piece of rock that he used as a mallet. He successfully avoided spilling any of the yet unknown contents. Tapping a barrel can go very wrong and is not a job for the inexperienced.

At last came the moment of truth – the long-awaited suspense and curiosity as to what the cask contained would soon be over. Surely it had to be whiskey! It was marked to contain thirty gallons, constructed of thick oak staves and bound with brass hoops. It seemed as if it had drifted in the ocean for a considerable time, where it accumulated a short, fuzzy, marine growth. This made it slippery and difficult to handle. Paddy held the tin mug while Jamesie opened the brass tap ever so easily. Soon a slender stream of dark, honey-coloured fluid gurgled slowly downward, until the tin mug was about half full. Jamesie said, 'It must be rum, it smells like wild honey.' Paddy dipped his forefinger in the liquid and proceeded to lick it like a cat, relishing each lick. 'Oh boy, but this is powerful stuff', he said.

Jamesie who could contain himself no longer, brought the mug to his lips and took a deep slug whereupon he immediately bent double, gagged and became breathless. He spluttered and coughed until finally regaining normal breathing, helped by Paddy's back-slapping. 'By God this is a dangerous brew, it has cleared the skin from my tonsils', exclaimed Jamesie. 'It must be diluted with three times as much boiling water.'

Paddy took a careful sip, saying, 'I feel it travelling out to the tips of my toes. It will make great punch. I love punch with lump sugar – you can't beat the P.P.'s nightcap.'

'Forget about your punch, we must decide how best to dispose of it, we can't drink a barrel of rum', said Jamesie. 'Furthermore, we must be careful with the sale – remember what happened to the barrels of lard, it could also happen to us. I don't want to wind up in court – jealous neighbours are bad news, boy.'

'Leave the sale of it to me', said Paddy. 'I have a plan.'

'It better be good', said Jamesie. 'I'm all ears.'

'We'll make a deal with Dan the Pedlar', continued Paddy. 'He's the safest man this side of the grave. He sells *poitín* at every fair in Kerry and was never pulled over yet.'

Now, Dan sold everything from flypaper to snuff, little bottles of seawater mixed with pepper and sugar as cough medicine. He sold a host of items, including *poitín*, for which he took secret orders. He never delivered the stuff himself but acted the perfect commercial traveller very successfully. The police never took him seriously, regarding him as a half-wit, which he feigned to an amazing degree of perfection. Having agreed to make a deal with Dan, Jamesie and Paddy both decided to call it a night. Putting the barrow inside the cave and carefully concealing the entrance with brambles, they walked together across the field. 'Your mother has light in her window yet. No doubt she'll want to know if we found something in the washtub. Don't let her smell your breath.'

When Dan the Pedlar was contacted, a bargain was drawn up and approved in strict secrecy. The rum was to be diluted and sold in bottles, half pint and smaller, containing one or two glasses each. These bottles could easily be concealed on your person. The half pint was sold at four shillings, the next, three shillings and the smallest for two shillings. Dan the Pedlar gave the new product a trade name of its own, as distinct from *poitín*, calling it 'American Moonshine'. Dan's reward was a third, as equal partner. The venture proved very successful. The beverage received a whispered acclaim among the 'under the counter' customers, a cure for almost any malady.

All went well, without a hitch, until the Feast of Michaelmas. Then came the first hiccup, which happened at a dance in a local country house. The large kitchen filled to overflowing with local folk and with pilgrims who usually came to pray at Saint Michael's Well on 'Pattern' (Patron) Day. They also took part in the ensuing mixture of revelry, dancing, drinking and praying. Among the crowd could be seen Dan the Pedlar, busily plying his wares with his usual stealthy confidence. American Moonshine was disposed of among pilgrim, prayerful and local faithful.

As the night wore on, nocturnal revelry reached a crescendo of sound – so much so, that the local RIC police on night patrol decided to investigate the source of the singing and shouting. To their consternation, they found many in various stages of intoxication. One youth had virtually fallen by the wayside; he had lost all orientation relating to the perpendicular. Footless and incoherent, he could only answer feebly, 'American Moonshine.' The police took him into custody, until he was sufficiently sober. When questioned as to where he acquired the alcohol, he vaguely remembered a stranger giving him a small bottle of what he termed American Moonshine. He told the police he saw everybody swigging it, but nobody seemed to know much about it, except for its name.

The police were not convinced. They took Dan the Pedlar in for questioning, all to no avail. Dan played the part of dreamy blankness to perfection, with an expressionless vacuity, giving answers so woolly and unrelated as to cause mirthful laughter among the questioning constables. The head constable was heard to observe, regarding the homeless 'knight of the roads', that he was 'either a confounding rascal or has a tin can and pebble for a brain.' Nevertheless the police searched the entire locality, every dyke and farmyard, excepting *Poll a' Chait*, which place was so obscured by undergrowth as to be unnoticeable.

Jamesie and Paddy decided to play 'possum' for a while, by suspending all commercial marketing of the American Moonshine Company until they felt sure all police activity had ceased. They would sneak into *Poll a' Chait* for a couple of hours each night, make themselves a mug of punch on a mini oil flame. Every rainy day they would retire to the cave, where they drank, smoked and slept comfortably on beds of dry withered bracken. In slang terms they were, 'having a ball' – what more could they ask for than owning their own 'local' and drinks for free? In a short time their capacity to absorb more alcohol became evident. They were under the spell of that powerful Greco-Roman deity called Bacchus.

All proceeded happily until Paddy's mother Sheila became uneasy and worried as to the whereabouts of Paddy and Jamesie, who had now been on the absent list for three long days and nights. As time went by, Sheila pondered on the best course of action to take, deciding as a first step she must notify the police of their disappearance, when, lo and behold, as she happened to glance momentarily through the kitchen window during her worried musings, she recognized the figure of her son staggering across the meadow in front of the house.

Paddy staggered to a halt, falling prostrate to the ground. His mother rushed to his aid uttering a startled cry. With all the strength of a loving mother, she helped him find his unstable footing, supporting each tottering step in his lurching gait, until she laid him on the kitchen settle. Two neighbours arrived at the same time. One carried the semi-conscious Jamesie on his back, helped by Dan the Pedlar. They laid him on a rug spread on the kitchen floor. Dan the Pedlar assured Paddy's mother that all would come right, saying they had only a drop too much and he had already ordered the doctor. Jamesie was incoherent and rambling, but two words were clear among the disjointed verbiage: 'American Moonshine'. When the doctor arrived he pumped out the excess alcohol from the tanks and administered an antidote to counteract toxic poisoning. After a bout of vomiting and concurrent explosions of superfluous gas from their exhaust valves, they both improved rapidly.

When Sheila was made aware of the full story and where the cask was hidden, she ordered Dan the Pedlar to bring the pickaxe saying, 'You plot-scheming old shagger, come with me to *Poll a' Chait*.' Dan knew better than to risk the ire of obduracy personified, so he obeyed meekly, despite his feeble protestations to save some of the blessed stuff. He watched the Amazonian Sheila reducing the cask to a little heap of staves and brass hoops with each swing of the heavy pickaxe, leaving the amber liquid flow into the ravine. Thus ended the commercial venture of the beachcombers.

# V

## *Old Worlds and New*

## SKELLIG MICHAEL IN
## THE LOBSTER SEASON

I always enjoyed lobster fishing in summer and early autumn, by the side of the great Skellig Michael. For me personally it had an emotive influence. I felt the power and natural beauty of the place, so complete in colour and formation. Wild, savage beauty on the one hand, blending harmoniously with great beds of near-crimson sea pinks and cliff-dwelling clumps of brittle little white, yellow and blue flowers, filling the hollows and rock crannies between the stately spires of weather-worn multicoloured rock of slate blue and grey, including a mixture of brownstone and marble veins, iron and geodic rock crystals. The brittle flowers I have referred to, a lightkeeper told me that climbers called them 'dead men's flowers'.

The approach to the rock on a sunny day presents a picture of colour only to be found in the secluded bowers of isolated nature, exuding tranquillity and sheer beauty. The various sea-fowl flitting lightly among the rocky peaks or nesting in the caves, give evidence of a constant sustenance of life and order, combined with an aura of peace, unbroken by the intrusion of man.

Remembering a day in my youthful thirties, while ashore on the Skelligs, I rested on a lofty rock ledge overlooking the Blue Man's Cave where I could gaze down into the clear green depths, to where the water was calm and lightly ruffled. I noticed a school of mackerel circling and also hundreds of glossan pollock moving very slowly, while in another cave near at hand, a school of porpoise seemed to be either hunting or playfully cavorting, puffing and diving, never leaving a seemingly chosen area. Several great black-backed gulls stood on points overlooking the marine display, as if in total indifference. I suddenly became aware of a puffin flying in from sea and heading straight toward me, only to land on the ledge just an arm's length away.

Now, I had read about St Francis and his way with birds and wild animals, but other than that, the good saint and I had nothing in common. For a while I was afraid to move or breathe lest I disturb my feathered companion. At the same time I couldn't help admiring the perfect colour scheme nature had arranged for its plumage. The creature seemed to accept me as another wild species, an appraisal I would be happy to get away with. The bird completely ignored my intrusion into its domain. I thought – was this the land of ultimate bliss where the lion shall lay down with the lamb? Strive as I may to become a lamb, the transition would only be miraculous.

But what has all this got to do with lobster fishing? Where you have sea and rocks you are sure to find seabirds, but as the wise old fisherman said, '*Ní fios cá bhfaighfeá gliomach*', 'You can never be sure where you'd find a lobster.' It was during the lobster season that I was able to observe more closely the great rock in all its aspects, and above all, its crowning glory – the old-world monastery, a masterpiece of its time and an inspiration of wonder. Every quarried stone, from the heavy slab to the rough splinter spoil, found a place in the scheme. Hundreds of tons of stone were quarried, lifted and carried and set by skillful artisans who must have worked like Trojans. They built walls of dry stone on the edge of overhanging cliff-face, which have stood the test of centuries. Theirs was undoubtedly a labour of love. They were craftsmen whose ancestors had emerged from the Stone Age. They evidently wanted to get away from the hurly-burly of the world, seeking the peace which the risen Christ had promised when he said, 'The peace I leave you is not of this world.'

Alas, their dream of seclusion and peace was rudely shattered in the ninth century, by the plundering greed of the Northmen.

The beehive, dome-shaped cells, completely habitable, leave a legacy to be marvelled at. The completed settlement, surrounded by an outer rampart of solid stone wall protecting and enclosing the entire structure, was at the time a massive undertaking. The evidence is to be found in the amount of work left behind by those early Christian monks, suggesting that occupation and construction on Skellig Michael started at a very early date and spread over many centuries – therefore, perhaps it is safe to assume that Rome wasn't built in a day.

Another distinctive feature of the rock is its two lighthouses, one now electronically controlled from the mainland. The earlier lighthouse, built up high on the north-west corner, was abandoned. It is suggested that early mariners complained of the lamp being often obscured by low cloud.

Now I must return to the realm of a lobsterman, and to the reality of hard work, and as this document relates to fin, fur and feather, give variety to the menu by adding plenty of shellfish. Lobster traps must be baited and set in the most likely ground, usually by the side of the reef which extends westwards from Skellig Michael called 'The washerwomen', or *Na mná* in Irish. In the twenties and thirties the reef teemed with red crayfish. Now, as a result of over-fishing, illegal diving and nets, crayfish will soon become an endangered species.

In those days we carried eighty large unwieldy barrel-traps that today would be considered old-fashioned in comparison with modern equipment. Our ropes were fibre grass, which chafed and raised blisters on our hands. Mechanical winches were unheard of in our neck of the trade. When hauling by hand in deep water, all that was required was a strong back and a weak mind. We overcame the chafing somewhat by improvisation, using old part-worn woollen socks as mittens, cutting a hole for the thumb.

Now, what would a fisherman wish to find in a trap? Lobsters and crayfish, of course, but if wishes were lobsters, a fisherman could become a wealthy merchant perhaps. But woe betide, this is not always the case. The worst and most unwelcome freeloader of all is the conger eel, a dangerous powerful marauder causing havoc and disruption to the fishing gear. In those days we didn't have a market for red edible crab, which were most numerous, and are up to the present plentiful.

All the species I have found in tidal rock pools and have already mentioned, come as unwelcome guests to dine at the lobsterman's expense. Tonight I will overhaul my lobsterpots, evict unwanted tenants, and replace torn or missing baits. I must use a number of different fish pieces to attract lobster. Salted mackerel is my first choice, but alas congers love salt mackerel and so I must use other fresh bait like pieces of fat bollan wrasse, which we get in our trammel net; fresh gurnard we get from the trawlers. Small flatfish, any kind of bait, scraps of fish not used for sale; I have tried pieces of meat, and portions of conger eel, and parts of drowned seafowl. Meat seemed to be rejected by the most voracious freeloaders who frequented our lobster table. Now, having prepared our traps, let us set them in the most likely places for the evening, to dusk haul. The lobster is a hermit, but will sally forth if attracted by the smell of bait in twilight.

It was an evening to remember, sixty-five years ago. Jim brought the *Island Rover* to a gentle stop in shelter of the 'Blue Man', telling me to cast the mooring stone, the great ocean like a millpond. It seemed so unreal, as if all nature was resting. The boat swung gently to the mooring, the only sound the gurgling ebb and flow of the darkening water between the rock fissures in the caves.

We put the kettle on and made ourselves mugs of nice hot tea, with delicious crab claws and slices of boiled crayfish tail, not forgetting homemade bread and butter. It was our usual cheap fare, but this evening, somehow, it seemed special. Then Jim said suddenly, 'We'll lay our head, before we make the last haul.' Ah, but Jim was like Napoleon, who had only to hit the pillow and was gone. The last rays of a declining sun filtered like threads of gold, as if sown specially, through the 'Needle's eye' and into the valley of 'Christ's saddle', lighting up the ramparts of the old monastery, casting a last soft glow of lingering light along the south face of the rock. I couldn't sleep – perhaps not tired enough to relax – looking up at the old settlement walls and listening to the plaintive calling of roosting kittiwakes, mixed with the lone-call of a passing gull. I could not help thinking of how many beautiful evenings such as this, centuries ago, did the monks of Skellig Michael chant their evensong of prayer in praise of the Risen Christ.

This poem for the occasion, I dedicate to my skipper, Jim Fitzgerald.

## The Last Haul

At last, a gentle silver mist
Shuts out
The torment of my brain
And like a child
Rocked in a chariot
Of sleep,
Sweet peace
Begins to reign.

I listened
To the vesper song
Slice through
The twilight eve
And kneeling there
Within their shadowed cells
I thought I heard
The hooded men
With upraised palms
Tell Christ
We owe you love.

I listened
To the kittiwakes complain
Within
The Blind Man's Cave,
The clamping
of the Northman's oars,
The stealthy rush
Ashore,
The clash of axe and spear,
A warrior
Of flaxen hair,
A stolen
Golden cup

*Held in his grasp.*
*And all is peace*
*Once more*
*Until I hear Jim call,*
*'Awake, it's the last haul.'*

Skellig Michael was plundered three times by the Vikings in the ninth century, eventually forcing the decimated order to abandon the rock and build the Priory called St Michael's near Horse Island. It is ironic, and interesting also, to note that what the Danes failed to achieve in the ninth century, Elizabeth I and Cromwell carried out on a more grandiose scale of total suppression and annihilation. The last Franciscan monk was captured and beheaded on Scarriff Island in Ballinskelligs Bay by Cromwellian forces, bringing monastic Christianity in Ireland to face a grim future. The Ireland of saints and scholars became engulfed in the funeral pyre of Saint Oliver's firebranding yeomanry. The Priory at Ballinskelligs, known to us today as the Abbey, was razed to the ground and its monks exterminated.

# PLACENAMES OF THE SKELLIGS SHORE

Placenames, like old family heirlooms, should be treasured and stored in the archives of our educational institutions, and revealed to our students from time to time. Placenames are not new – most of our names go back to before the advent of Christianity. Some names have deep roots in history, telling of battles, heroic deeds, mythical warriors, invasions, pagan ritual, etc.

The placenames I wish to present to the reader belong to the rock-bound coast of South Iveragh. Names of caves, reefs and cliffs which I took from my father and mother, I now take to be part of my heritage. Perhaps they were unaware of the legacy they were handing down, and I'm afraid a wealth of information is covered by the grave slab.

On the headland of Scariff Island, a reef comes up out of the deep to a height of sixty feet above sea level. Because of their natural formation, they appeared like a group of wooden wedges driven into the sea. The Irish name for the reef is *Na Deanncacha* – the Scariff wedges. Scariff Island takes its name from the Irish word *garbh*, meaning 'rough or wet territory'.

The first cave on the face of Scariff headland is called *Cuas na nDrisleoga*, 'the cave of the briars'. Why briars should grow on the barren exposed windswept cliff is beyond me.

The next cave, *Cuas an Chopair*, takes its name from a blue-green vein of copper ore evident on the rock face from the top of the cliff to under the sea. The copper cave lends its name to the geology of the island. The next point is an overhanging cliff called in Irish *An Cromán* – 'the hip'; in human terms it could mean the quarter. The next cave is called *Cuas an tSolais* – 'the cave of light'. The rock formation is like a one-arch bridge built against the cliff; the light tends to shine through the eye of the arch, hence its name. The exact same rock formation happens on the north-west side of the Small Skelligs, with the very same bridge structure, and light. Although twelve miles apart, the Great Artist, it is apparent, worked on both projects simultaneously, using time, erosion, wind and water as the tools of His trade.

On the north side, near the middle of the island, the rock face slopes gently down to the water's edge, making it easy to go ashore. This hollow is called *Clais na nÉamh*, and would mean 'the hollow of the groans', or it may refer to the word *naomh*, and mean 'the hollow of the saints'. Perhaps it has something to do with a giant's grave on the cliff top. The next cave is *Cuas an Bháid* – 'the boat cave'. Then we have *Bealach Scarbh*, the gap between Deenish Island and Scariff Island; 'Deenish' comes from the Irish words *dubh,* 'black', and *inis,* 'island', hence Black or Brown Island.

The island itself has a large area of barren rock, only a few acres of grazing land, and a small pebble beach. A family lived there until the Great War in 1914. A reef on the eastern tip of Deenish

has a strange name – *Na Glaibhinní*. Some say the word has a con-
nection to the French *'glaive'* for 'broadsword'.

Coming across to the headland on the southern side of Ballinskelligs Bay, there stands *Ceann Muice*, Hog's Head. The reef, a few
cable lengths outside the nose of the Hog, is called *Magairle na
Muice*, or 'the pig's testicles'. Two other rocks near the cliff-face are
known as *An Seanduine* and *An tSeanbhean*, 'the Old Man' and 'the
Old Woman'. A cave on the south side is *Cuas an Ghabhair*,
'Goat's Cave'. Two other caves are *Cuas Mór*, 'the large cave', and
*Cuas beag na Muice*, 'the little pig's cave'. It is interesting to see evidence of the Ice Age on the headland. Large square blocks of stone
weighing several tons sit precariously on the bare green fields on
the edge of the cliff as if dropped from the sky.

The word 'reen' is from the Irish word *rinn*, denoting a reef,
and is used in general, being applied to townlands such as
Reenard, Reenroe, Rinneen, etc. The next point east of Hog's
Head is called Rinneen Point, and the curve of the shoreline is
named *Lúb an Rinnín*, 'the Loop of Rinneen'. 'The point of the
reeds' stands out on the eastern corner of the loop – *Pointe na
mBioraí*, meaning 'thatching reeds or bulrushes'.

Next comes Rinneen Strand. Under the townland of Rinneen is
*Trá na Spáinneach*, 'the Spanish Strand', and the rock in front is
named *Carraig Oisín*, 'Oisín's Rock' of Celtic mythology. Oisín
was spirited to the Land of Youth by Niamh Chinn Óir on her
fairy steed. A nice name for a rock, but I was disappointed to learn
that more than one Oisín's Rock can be found on the southern
coast of Ireland.

Next in line is 'the Red Cliff', *An Fhaill Dhearg*, and the rock
that stands in front of Waterville village is *Carraig Éanna*, which is
linked in history with the coming of the Milesians, where it is said
Ír and Éanna, both sons of Milesius, came ashore. Waterville is a
name given to the village by the Normans, and later by the Pala-
tine planters. The original name of *An Coireán*, 'the whirlpool', or
'weir', from which it is derived, is the correct old placename.

Continuing north along 'Inny Strand', *Tráigh na hAoine*, there
is a submerged reef called 'The Blue Boys'. The old placename is

*Na Fir Ghorma.* Then we have the townland of *Muiríoch,* meaning 'land near a beach or a strand'. It has a long stretch of sand dunes; with the placename *Corcacha an Mhuirígh* – 'sand dunes or marshes'. Next is *Béal Átha an Inne,* 'the mouth of the River Inny ford'. On the north bank of the ford we have a two-mile stretch of beach running parallel to the Emlagh townlands. The word in Irish is *imleach,* meaning 'on the rim, edge, margin or border'; in this case the townlands bordered the sea: *Imleach na Muc* ('of the pigs'), *Imleach Draighneach* ('of the sloe tree / blackthorn'), *Imleach Mór* ('the big emlagh').

Part of the beach is *Tráigh na Sasanach,* referred to in history as 'The Englishman's garden', where an armed force was repulsed and defeated by the Irish peasantry when Sir Richard Denny failed to seize by force the local herds of cattle at the order of Queen Elizabeth the First.

The townland of *Rinn Rua,* meaning 'the red reef', is adjacent to *Abha an Churraigh* 'the river of the wet bog land', which enters the sea at the eastern end of *Mill a' Ghóilín* strand, *mill* or *meall* meaning 'a little hill or knoll', *góilín* 'a neck or inlet by the sea'. On the west we have *Cloch an Chófra,* 'the rock resembling a trunk or a box'. Then we come to the first of the caves on the *Dún Géagáin* side of Ballinskelligs Bay, *dún* meaning 'a fort or fortress'; but there remains a void in folklore as to who Géagán was or represented. Perhaps *géagán* here simply indicates an arm of the sea, referring to no one in particular.

The first cliff-face with a little boat cove is called *Faill an Rois,* which got its name from the wild flax – *an líon bréagach, bréagach* means 'not true flax'; *ros* means 'fairy flax'. Next is 'Hector's Point', *Pointe Hector,* which got its name from a Scottish family who settled there in the seventeenth century. Then comes *Cuas an Airgid,* where the pirate ship *Hercules* was wrecked with its 'silver' cargo.

Farther west is 'the Otter's Cave', *Cuas an Mhadra Uisce,* and 'the Cave of the Brown Sea Algae', *Cuas an tSleabháin* (a brown, edible seaweed). Around the corner is the 'Cave of the Chough', which is related to the crow family, hence the name in Irish – *Cuas na Cáige.*

Now we arrive at Ballinskelligs Strand, which in olden times carried the name of *Tráigh an Ghleanntáin*. At its eastern end is the *Bearna Dhearg*, which had a place in folklore, telling of a nocturnal ghostly equestrian who galloped furiously along the hard, sandy beach on moonlit nights, the beating of hooves echoing in the night air. The old tale referred to him as *Marcach na Bearna Deirge*, 'the Rider of the Red Gap'. Part of the mossy green beach running westward bore a very ancient placename, *Cnocán na mBuachaillí*, 'the Knoll of the Boys', where the clash of the ash, the laughter and support for the invisible sporting boys, called the *Slua Sí* or 'fairy host', was heard. *Cnocán na mBuachaillí* – what a pity we do not hear them play anymore.

Near the ruins of the old monastic abbey, the Priory, from which the parish takes its name – *an Phriaracht*, otherwise known as Ballinskelligs Abbey (*Mainistir Mhichíl*), was occupied by monks of Skellig Michael as early as the eighth century. Owing to severe coastal erosion at this point, many old placenames have vanished and are now no longer to be seen as points of identification. Gone is the pebble strand we called the *Bréitse* – 'the pebble foreshore'; gone is the *coinigéar-conneigire* – 'rush-grown beach'; gone is the *Cusbal/Cusbao* – 'calm tidal lagoon'; gone is *Bearna na gCorp* – entrance to the Abbey graveyard where the dead were left to be buried in 1847. Gone too is the *Seanphóna*, 'the old pound', a place for keeping trespassing cattle or cattle whose owners refused to pay their dues to the monastery, and *Púicín na gCeann*, 'the place of the skulls'.

Several acres of land with these placenames have disappeared from the local scene during my lifetime, because of constant erosion by the sea. This is why I wish to place on record many old placenames that have been lost or forgotten in the passage of time.

We will now go across Ballinskelligs Harbour to 'Horse Island', *Oileán na gCapall*. Why it was called Horse Island I do not know, except that we have other islands on the coast of Ireland which carry the same name. Two families, the Barrys and the Fitzgeralds, occupied the island until the late fifties. The land was poor and exposed to the harsh weather conditions, especially in wintertime.

It was no longer possible to keep in step with modern amenities on the mainland.

The people have marched on into a new technological world, but the Irish placenames of centuries remain behind as a memorial to their Gaelic culture. We have *Cois an Oileáin* – 'the foot of the island', *An Banc Bán* – 'the white sandbank', *An Drom* – 'the back of a place or a knoll', *Lochán na nDonnán* – 'pool of the rock ling', *Cuaisín an Ghrin* – 'Little Cave of the Gravel', *Leac an tSaighne* – 'flagstone of the seine net'.

On the south side of the island we find also a wealth of Irish names like *Leac na bhFachán* – 'flagstone of the periwinkles', *Cuas na Leacach* – 'cave of the flagstones', *Cuas an tSéideacháin*, an underwater cavern that ejects the seawater violently from its entrance. Next we have *Pointe an Fhionnaidh*, 'Fur Point', perhaps because it is a favourite place for sea otters that come ashore to clean and dry their fur. *Clais an Lochain, Clais Rua, Pointe Buí*, denote 'the hollow of the little rock pools', 'the brown hollow' and 'the yellow point'.

On the western head of Horse Island is a detached rock called *Na Fiacla*, 'the teeth', and a cave called *An Cuas Mór*, 'the Big Cave' where the grey stork makes a nesting place. *Carraigh na bPollóg*, 'Pollock Rock', and *Céim*, meaning 'a step', are nearby. Some of the island's fields also have names, such as *páircín*, 'little park', *An Stráice Caol*, 'the narrow streak field', and *Páirc an Tobair*, meaning 'the field of the well'.

The island sound is called *Bealach an Oileáin*. On the north side is the townland of Reen (*Rinn*), meaning 'a reef or stony ground'. The cliff-face extends westward to Bolus headland, and around into St Finan's Bay to Valentia. The great cliffs stand in unbroken sequence, wild and imposing in splendour, on the other hand, awesome and formidable.

The cliffs I have become familiar with during my life as a fisherman were known to me only by Irish placenames, which go back to our Gaelic ancestors. Some placenames have baffled historians and experts as to their meaning. Perhaps rocks were named before books were written. One of the many caves on the Reen-side is

*Cuas Elinore.* Who Elinore was is not known, a lover of some poet, no doubt. Then we have the headland called *Cloigeann an Chrainn* – 'head or skull of the wild cats'.

Several caves take names suggested by their shape or natural outline, others from bird life, or perhaps some event in history. We have 'the cave of the peat', *Cuas na Móna, Cuas na gColúr*, 'cave of the pigeons', *Carraig an Staighre*, a cliff-face, with a perfect stair formation, *Cuas an Iallait*, 'Cave of the Saddle', *Cuas na Gaoithe*, 'cave of the wind', *Creatlach*, 'headland', *An Chráiteach*, meaning that a tormented choppy sea was usually experienced when passing by the head.

Two rocks face the entrance to Boolakeel Strand; one is the *Gamhnach*, meaning 'a milch cow', and the other is *An Mheadar*, meaning 'the churn'. *Cuas na Léime*, 'the cave of the leap' – in folklore it is said a person escaped from his pursuers by leaping across the chasm. Several old names apply to rocks and reefs near the ancient townland of *Cill Rialaig*. The real meaning of the Irish name is only a matter of conjecture. The answer is blowing in the wind. It was home to Séan Ó Conaill, storyteller extraordinaire, who told stories to himself in the fields when his audience diminished.

Another name from the past is *Ceann an Aonaigh*, 'the headland of the fair', or *Aonach*, no doubt going back to the druids. Overlooking the headland is a *cathair* with ogham symbols. Another reef is named *Scoth na hEaglaise*, whose derivation or origin has faded from memory. Nearby is a rock called *An Scéalaí*, 'the storyteller'. When certain signs of surf or currents were seen near the rock, it meant the rock was giving a weather forecast, telling a story of the weather.

*Carraig na bhFiach*, 'the rock of the raven'; *Leac na mBeathach*, 'the flagstone of the good yield'. *Beatha* in this case meant that an angler fishing from *Leac na mBeathach* would be rewarded. *Cuas an Daimh*, 'the Cave of the Ox', *Cuas an tSeaga*, 'the Cave of the Cormorants', *Faill an Reithe*, 'the Cliff of the Ram', *Carraig Dhaingean na nGabhar*, 'the rocky fortress of the goats': all these caves and many more are to be seen on the cliffs leading westward to Bolus Head. I mention only interesting features such as 'the

Pedlar's Box', *Bosca an Pheidléara*, a cube of polished rock totter-ing on the lip of a precipice; and 'Pipín's Cave', called *Poll Pipín*: Pipín, in local folklore used the cave as a hideout to evade the au-thority of the law; *Boilg Thomáis*, the reef of Thomas, and 'the great sunken reef', on the head of Bolus – *An Charraig Shuncáilte*, *bólus* meaning 'a cowherb'.

The cliffs between Bolus and Duchealla headlands are steep and precipitous, wildly beautiful and still exuding a savage pristine pic-ture of an era when both time and matter merged. Within this kingdom of surging mighty Atlantic sea is found a haven of refuge to many creatures – herds of grey Atlantic seals and seabirds – that survive and renew the order of their species, year after year, re-sponding to some inborn power which I, myself, for want of a bet-ter explanation, call instinct. *Dúchealla*, means 'the black cells': the origin of what the black cells were is unknown.

Now I will pass by Dúchealla headland and enter St Finan's Bay. The first placenames on the starboard side are 'Cave of the Bald Knoll', *Cuas an Mhaoláin*, then the *Lícín Rua* or the 'Brown flat rock'. Next is a rock feature called *Láimh Cláir*. I do not know the origin of this very old name meaning perhaps 'a wooden hand'.

Then we come to a series of teeth-like rocks barely showing above the surface of the sea, in off-circular formation, resembling rock pools. The apt Irish name given here is *Na hUmaracha*, mean-ing 'the wells', a place to be given a wide berth by the night fish-erman. Then we have the 'Devil's Cliff', or *Faill an Deamhain*, where it is said in folklore that a man from Ballinskelligs wrestled with the demon on the cliff top. There is also the 'Cave of the De-scent', or 'resembling a slipway', *Cuas an Fháin*, and 'the slender reef', *An Rinn Chaol*. Next we have a nasty sunken rock called *Builg an Phríosúin*, 'the Prison Rock'; then *Ceann Garbh*, meaning 'the rough point', and *Rinn an Chaisleáin* – *caisleán* meaning 'cas-tle'. Perhaps the reef gets its name from a landlord's eighteenth-century house on the nearby townland, now a ruin.

Then we have *Leac na mBan*, the flat rock where it is said three women were drowned (the date is not known) while collecting limpets, hence, 'the Women's Flagstone'.

Under the townland of Tooreen, *tuairín* or 'turret', we have 'the Cave of Paddy Bhuí', and *Cuas an tSrutháin*, 'Cave of the Stream,' where the four-masted sailing ship, the *Nielsen Hauge,* referred to earlier, was wrecked in the nineteenth century with a full cargo of pine wood. The ship was in perfect condition, all sails set, no living person on board except for a scrawny cat. Many such ships were abandoned in the Atlantic in mysterious circumstances. Under the townland of *Athghort,* meaning 'a garden being tilled continually', we have a little corner-strand of rounded stones called *Trá Leagaídh.* I do not know the meaning of the name, except at this point a cairn of stones is seen in memory of a priest who, according to folklore, was slain there. To the north of this is 'Keel Strand', *Trá na Cille,* also known as St Finan's Bay, a wild Atlantic beach with high-rolling breakers, suitable for surfboarding but dangerous for swimmers, owing to violent undertow.

The townland of Faha, *Faich* – denoting an even, grassy strip of ground without humps – was a playing pitch in early writing. Underneath Faha the cliff-face is much lower. Here we find lovely old Irish names like *Dúna* and *Puicín an Tobac* and *Caladh an Bháid.* Reaching westward are the pleasant slatey cliffs of Moyrisk, *Maothroisc,* until we come upon Puffin Island sound, immortalized in a poem by the Iveragh poet Tomás Rua Ó Suilleabháin. The sound is called *Bealach na nÉamh,* 'the Gap of Sighs'. *Oileán na gCánóg,* Puffin Island, is now a national bird sanctuary. *Ceann Dubh,* or 'Black Head', stands high and deep at its western end. Two and a half miles west is the bald lone rock of *Lomán,* bastardized as Lemon Rock. *Lomán* comes from the word *lom* meaning 'bare'.

I owe a special debt of gratitude to my parents, who spoke the ancestral language to us when we were children. The music of the tongue mixed naturally with the growing pains of our adolescence, giving us the status of native Irish speakers.

I remember listening spellbound to my mother telling me the story about 'the Island of the Fairy Women', or 'the Foolish Wife and the Golden Shoe'. My father, on the other hand, bestowed on me the wealth of these resonant Irish placenames that are fast vanishing from the spoken language of a new generation.

## THE SOFT SOUTH WIND OF SKELLIGS

Never was a day more to my liking than when soft zephyrs sang from the south, blowing gently across the bay of Skelligs whose waters reflected an azure sky adorned with the fluttering white of the gull's wing. It was the threshold of a new summer, a time to be glad. I could feel the life-giving energy of the great ocean, which seemed to enter my very being, calling nostalgically – come away … come away …

Glittering rays of morning sun sparkled, spilled and splashed from wavelet to wavelet and onto the back of a slow heaving billow that arose lazily from the depths of a mighty bosom. Lesser gulls wearing white aprons and little black caps, were scattered like 'sea daisies' across the blue-green fields of the bay. Some birds seemed to hang suspended above the waters, their wings a special whiteness unlike the whiteness of snow – a colour which stood out to me and could be seen flashing against a background of blue. Even away in the distance their wings seemed like a glint of white lightning in the sky. Black guillemots and razorbills called in shrill voice, singing or composing poems, diving and reappearing from the spume white froth, their bills laden with silver sprat.

On a day such as this could be heard the music of the ocean, the deep throated husky laugh of that fickle monarch of the deep, the sea god Poseidon, who might fume and fluster into a raging tempest or wear the smile of an infant in the cradle of a May morning.

As the sail filled with a belly full of freshful fragrance, I could feel the tautening of the canvas when the little boat comes alive, leaning her shoulder against the sudden rush of water from her bow wave, leaving a furrow in her streaming wake like a ploughshare in the blue field of the bay.

Congregations of screaming Arctic terns with scissor-pointed wings swooped, plunged and dived for their share in the fruits of the kingdom, where myriads of silver sprat had surfaced, much to their excited delight.

Puffins with their multi-coloured beaks, like circus clowns breaking the water, and little auks and crossbills all feasted at nature's free table, provided for their survival.

Little white clouds like puff balls of thistledown danced ballet across the blue ceiling of the sky. All things alive and life in all things. Praise the Lord for the resurgence of life I felt around me and in my very soul that morning when the soft south winds sang across the bay of Skelligs.

The molten mirror of the sun trundled its fiery wheel across the southern sky, climbing the ladder of infinity and marking the milestone of yet another day. The grey blue rock of the holy hermits, Skellig Michael, standing sentinel by the Kerry headlands came into view, as we swept by the wild head of Bolus out into open sea, where the south wind took on a more lively singing note, causing the boat to dance and increase in speed, tossing her bow over little hummocks of water which laughed and sparkled in her sea way, throwing white blossoms of spray aboard as if to bless her.

Out here all things lived. Ronan the seal played and revelled in the churning surf. An ugly, hook-beaked cormorant pointed its tail feathers heavenwards disappearing beneath the green waters. Manx shearwaters skimmed the surface. Together with the swallow-like flight of the grey fulmar, the great solan goose, mighty bird of the Atlantic, flew towards Little Skelligs, bearing a long streamer of bladder wrack in its great beak, the building material of a new nest, in expectation of this year's offspring. Little dolphins puffed and played, racing alongside, looping, bending and curving their sleek forms, perhaps in wonderment of man and his little boat.

On a morning such as this what would I wish for? Swallow wings! Yes, swallow wings, wished for by a mere mortal who would feign divest himself of all earthly inhibitions.

I have looked upon the great water asleep like a smiling infant in a cradle, only to awaken to a rosy dawn to watch white horses charging across the bay. I have witnessed sunsets leaving a golden staircase painted on the wave, leading to a flaming crown of molten gold hanging momentarily on the horizon. I can only say – who is the artist? If it be you, oh God, then thank you!

## THE SEA IN HIS BLOOD

Together with other boys from the neighbourhood, we sailed little boats, assembled from green *feileastram* fronds, held together by prickly furze thorns. What fun it was to watch our little green ships steer an erratic course across the placid face of the duck-pond at the foot of the meadow, while frolicsome summer zephyrs determined the course of each unpredictable voyage.

I also looked longingly towards the harbour beneath our townland; often in wondrous awe did I watch the towering blue-green billows between Horse Island Sound and the mainland rise up, up and ever upwards, like a performing circus stallion, until the white frothing lip of the mighty breaker came boiling over, slowly curling downwards with a mighty thunderous boom, filling and spilling a crazy volume of tormented water into the harbour's mouth.

'He had the sea in his blood.' Every so often do I hear a father or mother give utterance to these words speaking of a sailor son who'd answered the call of the sea. It was put beautifully by John Masefield in his poem 'Sea Fever' from *Salt-Water Ballads* (1902):

> *I must go down to the seas again,*
> *For the call of the running tide,*
> *Is a wild call and a clear call,*
> *That may not be denied.*

True words, that mysterious inexplicable force which arouses curiosity and suspense, calling for a journey into the unknown. Such is the powerful attraction the poet so aptly describes.

This could also be attributable to my own people. My brother John joined the navy at the age of sixteen; another two brothers went steamboating to foreign parts, as able seamen. Men who follow the sea are often found to be quaint, having unusual and perhaps odd beliefs. I knew one such gentle seaman who had spent most of his life afloat. He always kept the crown of his head tonsured, then a ring of hair plaited into little pigtails hanging over a lower shaven ring, which he called a double tonsure. He completed the effect with large gold or ivory earrings. This hairdo was in vogue during the pirate period.

To most deep-water sailors the sea is regarded as a fickle mysterious sorceress, a mistress both bountiful and unfaithful, with ever-changing whims and vagaries. Therefore, despite new technology, sailor men still harbour within themselves a certain superstitious respect for the mighty ocean.

Deep-water men are superstitious, believing in signs and omens that seem to fill the vacancy left by the awesome nature of the great ocean. Long voyages are now very rare, as present-day ships have power, speed and all modern comforts. Despite all, the call of the sea remains, a longing to visit strange lands, to be out there alone, far from the madding crowd, with only the dark canopy of the sky studded with myriad fiery constellations.

The terrible feeling of complete aloneness is experienced by the lone voyager. Noises come in the darkness from the heaving hills of a seemingly boundless ocean. On a calm night can be heard the sudden explosive crash of disturbed water dislodged by the ponderous bulk of some huge denizen of the deep, or maybe a once off, sickening, human-like cough in the vicinity of the boat. Phenomena such as these serve only to add to the mystique of the ocean. Some men have sailed alone across the several oceans having endured privation, both mental and physical. Still, after only a short stay on shore they are already plotting the course of other such voyages.

The sailor's love is the sea; her breaking billows his serenading song of love, her heaving bosom his pillow, the careening deck and dancing prow his pride. He knows his boat as a lover knows his bride. She becomes all things to him, he knows her every whimsical movement in a seaway, be it fair or foul. He will guide her with steady hand among the furious frothing white-maned stallions of the storm that come charging down from the green-bellied mountains, shaking their hoary heads, rearing and snarling without rein or rider, derisively spitting white-raged froth at the man-child who has dared to lay claim to their territory

When the going gets tough he has one, or perhaps two, more aces up his sleeve. He will trim his bride down to storm wear, only little kerchiefs on bare poles; turn tail and run. Then the white steeds give chase once more, crashing, chasing and charging, trying in their fury to overwhelm. 'Run like the devil or do not run at all.'

Then comes the time when the last card must be played. The running is all over, to survive he must heave-to. He awaits his chance for a gap between the breaking billows. When he finds it, he must be quick. Helm hard over, he brings her head to wind and casts the sea anchor, paying out the line, fathom after fathom, while the little boat slips astern. The can of oil with its tiny puncture is hung overboard, night will soon be falling. She hangs well on the canvas cone. The big waves are not crashing aboard any more. The oil is doing its job, drip by drip marvellously calming the lip of each seething breaker.

The sailor breaks out a night storm lamp, also a red and green navigational light. He will slip below for a quick warm drink before coming on deck again to look the storm in the eye and share vigil with his sturdy boat. The wind has shifted a few points, making a witch's cauldron of jumping cross sea, causing the sea-anchor rope to whip dangerously. The moon shows momentarily through the broken cloud scud. My God! It scurries like a rat across a screen of torn cloud, appearing again and again at intervals. The cloud layer is not so dense. Later a sudden burst of moonlight shows on the turbulent, tormented horizon. It is only a game of waiting; the wind comes in fitful gusts. The heavy seas are losing their surface speed. The line to the sea anchor does not whip so much. The little craft hangs easier now. Two hours more of weary vigil. A cold dawn breaks. The sea is much smoother. He has slept in a sitting position, feeling cold and cramped. He hauls and stows the sea anchor, takes the can of oil on board, waits for sunrise to plot his position, shakes out his sails, rigs the tiller, hauls home the sheet, away again, pulling across a favourable breeze, perhaps to a land full of swallow wings.

Why does he do it? Why suffer another trip across this boundless waste? Maybe because he has the sea in his blood!

> *From Neptune's cup*
> *He quaffs,*
> *A draught of dreams*
> *Of lands beyond the bay,*
> *Where ocean streams*
> *Run swift,*
> *And gambolling dolphins play,*
> *Where nymph sprites strum*
> *The sailor's lyre of love,*
> *Within the shrouds*
> *He must not stay.*
> *So heave the halyard,*
> *And away.*
> *The sea is in his blood.*

## VOYAGE TO AMERICA

The local innkeeper was the owner of two small fishing vessels, manned and skippered by local crews. The hours were from dawn to midnight. No fish meant no pay. The crew supplied their own food: boiled fish, bread and tea. All work, such as scrubbing the hulls, repairing, painting, wintering and mending gear, was not considered by the owners as work to be paid for. Took what you got and asked no questions. The work was hard and backbreaking for the lack of power winches, only a crude windlass for lifting a heavy trawl full of fish from thirty-five to forty fathoms of water. Landing facilities were bad and hours unlimited, men often working a whole week of eighty hours for a pittance of fifty shillings. Conditions which smacked of the 'Georgia Chain Gang' left within me a feeling of being caught in a vicious poverty trap, or rather being owned, body and soul, by some set of unknown economic circumstances for the sake of my daily bread.

It was because of conditions such as I have described that I wished earnestly to escape. I wrote to my brother Timothy, who worked in Connecticut, asking him if he would help me to get to the United States. He kindly sent me the passage boat-fare, for which I was extremely grateful. I felt like the bird in the poem:

*I'm free, I'm free, I'll return no more,*
*My weary time in this cage is over.*

If only I had knowledge of what lay in store for me, I would also have a cure for all ills. This I take from an old saying in Irish, which I often heard from my mother, how true:

*Dá mbeadh fhios agam, bheadh leigheas agam.*

I was virtually jumping from my unhappy position in Ireland into the middle of a great depression – the Wall Street Crash. Having collected all the necessary documents required from Church and State by the US Department of Immigration, I was called to Cobh for a medical and mental scrutiny. I stayed at a hotel with other aspiring immigrants.

The morning was bitterly cold, with a light snow on the ground. Ten of us were ushered into a hall fitted with cubicles, and told to remove all our clothing. I was in the cubicle nearest the door, protected only by a flimsy screen. Being stark naked, I felt miserably cold. We had waited some time for the American doctor to arrive. I remember him dressed in white, jovial, smiling with dark, horn-rimmed spectacles. Glancing into my cubicle as he passed, he must have observed goose pimples, or perhaps a shiver.

He stopped suddenly and asked if I felt cold. I answered, 'Yes Sir.' He checked all the other cubicles and ordered heaters to be brought in, saying, 'These men are cold.' I was the first to be called. He made a quick check of my body, observing once more that I should put some clothing on in case of being chilled. After a quick reading and memory test, some mental arithmetic and inspection of personal underwear, he gave me a full okay on all grounds. When dressed, I waited my turn to appear before the American consul and staff, who stamped my passport and scrutinized my other documents. They asked me why I wished to emigrate. I replied that I had the intention of bettering myself and finding employment. They asked if I had a job waiting for me, to which I answered in the negative. After noticing the addresses of my relatives in the USA and that of my sister with whom I was to reside, I was given a visa and an immigration quota number, enabling me the legal right to enter, seek work and stay indefinitely in the USA.

I booked passage with the North German line, Hamburg American. It was an old liner, the S.S. *Dresden*, which took seven days to cross the Atlantic and which was taken out of service soon after. At this period, newer more luxurious and faster ships were contending for the blue riband of the Atlantic: mighty ships such as the S.S. *Rex*, *QE2*, S.S. *Bremen*, S.S. *Europa*, S.S. *Queen Mary*, S.S. *America*, and the S.S. *Andrea Doria*, which tragically sank in a collision in the North Atlantic, with loss of life .

Tearfully and reluctantly I said goodbye to my parents, who were now ageing. I was the last of seven to leave the little thatched cottage and the postage stamp sized farm of cutaway bog. The farm was divided into six one-acre lots among the rural and unsettled peasantry of South Iveragh. The resident landlord and his agent levelled an exorbitant rent on each holding, payable in half-yearly gales. Woe betide the tenant who was found in arrears; he could expect the sky for a roof and the roadside his garden.

Humble though our lot in life, the thatched cottage was our castle. Even in poverty we were proudly poor. Like our many good neighbours we had plenty of potatoes, cabbage, turnips, onions, eggs, milk and fish and also the love of a closely knit family who accepted and shared fortune or tribulation.

That January evening, as dusk was enveloping the receding shoreline behind the Fastnet Rock, the great ship seemed to gather speed, scattering the white-capped waves into spray and ploughing a giant furrow through the back of each approaching Atlantic billow. The last streak of cold winter sunlight illuminated the western horizon. A stiff westerly breeze was building up, carrying with it a sniff of approaching rain. I could enjoy each moment, each pulsating movement of the ship whose deck was vibrant beneath my feet, her great, white superstructure and bridge. I could visualise a wise and competent captain, nursing and gently guiding his beloved ship, bringing her safely through the awful fury of an Atlantic hurricane. Somehow, I felt a void in my heart that night. I was lonely; the mercury of ambition had plummeted. My old father was lonely. I could see it in his countenance, bereft of any emotion when I said goodbye. Mothers, too, suffer in loneliness and love for their offspring. The deck steward ordered us below. Just as well, I felt I had betrayed my parents in the selfish interest of self-betterment. I refused to feel sorry for myself.

Mike Moran, my school companion, and David Fitzgerald also travelled on the *Dresden*. We were all in the same boat, trying to adjust to whatever lay in store. The majority of the passengers were continental, Germans, Austrians and some Jews. We soon made friends with different people, some who were returning to the States.

On the second day the weather grew steadily worse, blowing a full gale. We were confined to the salons of the lower decks. Many passengers suffered from severe 'mal-de-mer'. Some were confined to their bunks. It was pitiful to see healthy folk vomiting all over the place. They showed a film for the passengers' entertainment in a small theatre. The theatre was almost empty, owing to seasickness. The breakfast table had many empty chairs. We got fillet of raw, salted herring rolled into a ball, and held with a wooden pin. Mike Moran tasted one, making a wry grimace in disgust. Paddy Brown observed, 'They must think we're cats, serving us raw fish.'

One American-born German returning from Hamburg to the USA on hearing Paddy's remark exploded into a convulsive fit of laughter, nearly choking and set us all into a laughing gag. One of the waiters asked, 'Vot is so vunny, zat you not like vish?'

We passed near a four-masted barque, beating her way westward, under shortened sail, a large ship, laden deeply. A sailing ship was becoming a rare sight on Atlantic routes. 'A tall ship and a star to steer her by', becoming ghost ships in the memory of seafarers.

The third day, the weather cleared; the face of the ocean appeared more placid and we were allowed on deck. Myriads of Manx and greater shearwaters, with undulating flight, were forever rising and falling in unison with the movement of the sea. Storm petrels like little black chicks with short, webbed, flat feet seemed to stand momentarily on the lip of a billow, scooping a microscopic droplet of rich plankton oil floating in the ocean. Nature provided a perfect spoon-recess on the lower bill for this purpose. Deep-sea sailors are highly superstitious regarding this beautiful, bat-like creature, the harbinger of storms and foul weather when the birds are seen to congregate in wisps. A wisp of petrels is three or more birds. From a fisherman's point of view, I could stand by the rail for long periods, being rewarded for my patience by observing a small school of flying fish scatter by, leaping into the wind with fins outstretched, awakened by the bow wave of the rushing, leaping bulk of an ocean liner. I often observed dolphins expose their blue-grey arching backs, and once a pod of small, black, spouting whale calves.

The voyage westward became more pleasant as the passengers found their sea legs. It was obvious that some German females and some young Irish Paddies became more and more interested in each other's companionship. Language didn't seem to create an insurmountable barrier to friendship. Three things that can be found anywhere in the world: an Irishman, a German woman and a Swedish matchstick.

High on the main mast, the crow's nest was manned night and day. There were also port and starboard lookout posts. Paddy

Browne from Clare had ginger hair, was five foot six inches tall, had blue eyes and was well-built. He was always neat, clean and well-groomed, a young, well-spoken, well-behaved man who nevertheless would call a spade a spade. A German girl, much his senior, took a liking to Paddy. She dressed in an untidy fashion, or so it seemed to him. Her dress hung wide and voluminous from beneath her arms to the floor, thus concealing entirely whatever footwear she wore. Her sleeves were filled at the wrists, her upper deck showed bulging breasts below a thick neck and square head, with a mop of flaxen, flowing hair. She haunted Paddy, hung on his shoulder and suggested she give him singing lessons. With a song that she had translated from German, called 'Apple Blossom Time', she would demonstrate her ability by placing one hand on Paddy's shoulder and using the other as if conducting a choir. She sang in a sweet voice:

> *I vill be wit you in apfel bloomen time,*
> *I vill be wit you to change your name to mine.*

Turning, she would say to Paddy, 'Now I teach you love song.' Paddy decided she was cuckoo, saying, 'If only I could say coo coo in German, I'd tell her so.' The boys would retort, 'Can't you give her an Irish cuckoo?' Whereupon Paddy would tell us all (in modern jargon) to 'piss off'.

As we got to know each other, we enjoyed the crack. One young man from another province was dubbed 'Sly Britches'. John Rodgers from Dundalk was an engineer and believed hydraulic power would play a great role in future industry. He was a kindly and serious person and an asset to the country of his adoption.

Another mysterious young man – whose name except that of William, I can't but remember. His hometown was Maynooth. He bore the hallmark of the academy or perhaps the boarding school. He was very fond of a dark, unclouded night, when the stars were blazing. His knowledge of astronomy was amazing. He educated both John Rodgers and myself, one starlit night, while we were walking the deck. He believed strongly, while expounding the

Darwinian theory, in the possibility of a non-existing supreme being, and that Galileo would be proven right. He lived, he said, in this agnostic and atheistic void and was perfectly happy. His love of poetry became evident, how beautifully he quoted lines to prove a point. Whether a spoiled priest or a professor, looking back, it was nice knowing him. It takes all kinds to make a world.

Maybe it was because we had lived together in the same 'house' for a whole seven days, that we became curious of our different traits and outlook on life. Although we were birds of a feather, we all seemed different. No doubt each individual became an object lesson to the other. One middle-aged man called 'Mack' was returning to the USA to live with his sole surviving daughter. He had been in the States in his youth and didn't relish the thought of ending his days there. He cherished the idea of coming back to a small holding that he still owned in Tipperary. He was convinced that there was no place like Tipp. A sad kindly man who recited the rosary and exhorted us to do the same, undoubtedly he had a great devotion to the Virgin. I only pray that he realized his wish and returned to the vales of Tipp.

Notices written in several languages were placed on the walls of all the salons and recreation rooms:

BEWARE OF PROFESSIONAL GAMBLERS,
PICKPOCKETS AND PROSTITUTES.

Someone asked Paddy Browne what the difference was between a gambler, a pickpocket and a prostitute, to which he replied, 'No difference at all, men – don't you know they're all hoors.'

Time went by quickly. The laugh and the crack were great, like all fleeting moments of happiness which seem to pass so quickly. As the S.S *Dresden* moved under reduced speed into the narrows, the great towering skyscrapers of Manhattan stood like giant monuments along the waterfront. It was a calm morning. There was an oily sheen on the face of the great port. Merchant ships with sirens blaring, entered and left, all observing the law required by the port authority. There were city council tugs towing a string of barges, full of litter to be dumped off the coast, fruit ships from the south, cruise liners with holiday makers bound for the sun, coastguard cutters, port police boats, luxurious yachts, fishing vessels, buoys and markers with port traffic lights for the mariners benefit. A pilot boat scurried alongside, a ladder-like gangway was lowered. An agile figure in blue uniform with gold braid jumped like a cat onto the ship's ladder. Making his way to the bridge, this man's job was the safe berthing of the ship. He was a professional port pilot. Two tugboats, which seemed so tiny, one at the bow and one at the stern, they mothered, pushed and puffed until the great ship lay safely berthed beside the pier allotted to her. All Irish passengers were assembled in a large office-like room on the liner, where an immigration official checked our passports, which seemed to be a formality. The medical examination was quick and efficient. This was carried out in case of an outbreak of disease during the voyage. We said goodbye on the dockside. I only met Mike Moran on two other occasions, once in New York and once when he visited Ireland. We were school companions and neighbours.

A returning Irish woman from Cavan joined me in sharing a taxi from the dockside to the vast Central Station. Here we took a train, which served all the shoreline stations from New York to Boston. The landscape was still gaunt and barren, recovering from the sub-zero temperatures of the New England winter. I noticed only small parcels of open countryside. The built up areas with many great chimneystacks suggested a highly industrialised country with a large population. I parted with Mrs Whelan at New Haven railroad station, which I was to know so well in the very near future. With brown suitcase in hand I walked through the station to the taxi rank outside. As I approached a uniformed driver, he immediately swung the door open for me. I said, 33 Wilson Street, which was my sister's and her husband Paddy Reardon's address. The taxi driver informed me of how difficult it might be to get work, owing to factories laying off staff and closing down. He painted a dismal picture of the approaching depression, saying, 'I guess you hit this country the wrong year, Irish!' How prophetic his words.

My sister Mary must have heard my footsteps on the raised veranda, with its rocking chair. Many must have mistaken me for a distant relation of the prodigal son, so embracingly emotional was her welcome. Having reached destination, 'Hope and Glory', I confessed I felt rather tired. Only at this juncture did I realize how misinformed I was in relation to the work problem in the USA. My sister Sheila, who lived nearby, came immediately to bestow on me her version of 'the prodigal welcome'. Thank God they didn't have a fattened calf, as the creature would surely have been sacrificed on the altar of ignorance, especially in regard to the Wall Street Crash.

Paddy Reardon came home from work at the storeroom of the New York – New Haven and Hartford railroad. After greeting me, he asked me a question, which in the first place caused me surprise, and at the same time, required a sudden decision. 'Mike, do you think you could turn out to work on the railroad at half-six tomorrow morning? The section boss asked me this evening if I knew of anyone who could fill a vacancy. It's hard work and only two dollars fifty a day. I said you were arriving this evening, so he told me to contact him on the phone. What do you say Mike, will you take the job?' I replied, 'Okay, I'll take what's offered.' Paddy contacted Mr Bernhardt, a German who had been working for the Canadian Pacific Rail Road. He was curt in his reply: 'Okay Pat, bring in the harp in the morning.' After a warm bath, I got to bed early, and Morpheus, that beautiful God of slumber, folded his gossamer wings across my tired eyes.

I must have slept like a log. I thought I heard Paddy's voice in the distance saying, 'Will you go to work Mike, or are you too tired?' 'Oh! Of course, of course', I said jumping up and rubbing my eyes, at five-thirty. Paddy had some porridge, coffee and rye bread ready for my breakfast. Mary had prepared some meat sandwiches for my lunch. It was as yet early morning and I remember we walked into Lambarton Street by the intersection of Howard Avenue. We passed the seamless rubber factory, through the watchman's gate of Yard Four Freight and Passenger Complex, which was the station house.

Paddy left me at a wooden hut-cum-office and tool house, situated on the waterfront. A rough, boarded floor with a large coal stove set in the centre with seating all around. Mr Bernhardt's roll-top writing desk with swivel chair occupied one corner. A burly figure, weighing at least two hundred and eighty pounds, dressed in a blue boiler suit, jacket and peaked hat, stood by the stove, cursing and muttering in broken sentences. I was left in his care by Paddy, who seemed to be an old friend of this huge, good-natured native of the Italian Tyrol. He poked and fussed with the coal stove, which seemed to lack a draught. Going outside, he returned with a long iron rod with which he riddled the grate violently. Suddenly, the flame sprung to life, the big man uttered an expression of satisfaction – 'Ah! I make you pull, you son of a bitch.' He then sat down and asked if Pat Reardon was married to my sister. 'Pat is a nice man.' He went on to say, 'This was good country, Mike, but Hoover ruin it. You only come from old country yesterday and get job today.' He chuckled with a suppressed half-laugh, half-cough, 'I'll be a son of a bitch, luck of the Irish.'

Mr Bernhardt, our boss, arrived in company with two other men who were permanent members of what was known in railroad terms as 'Section 4'. One was Frederick Breault, a French-speaking Canadian; another was Samuel Marks, son of an English father and an Irish mother, who to my astonishment was from our neighbourhood in Ireland. John de Maio, the big Italian, was our track-walker. He was nicknamed 'Jumbo'; Frederick was called 'Frog'; Sam was 'Bottle Arse'; and I was 'Green Harp'. We were responsible for the upkeep of the rails in the freight yard. Mr Bernhardt recruited me to the permanent gang, asked me to sign my name and gave me a brass cheque with my register number. Shaking hands, he said, 'Mike, I hope you become president of the railroad!'

The first day passed quickly. I got every assistance from my fellow workers on how to use the heavy tools: the heavy jack for lifting track, spike pullers, tamping irons, gauges, spiking mauls, Jim Crowes, etc. I walked back to 33 Wilson Street without losing my way. My sister viewed it as an intelligent achievement for a greenhorn.

The summer turned into a real scorcher with high temperatures and many violent thunderstorms. We never laid tools flat on the ground, as in a short time a bar would become too hot to handle.

Freddie Breault and myself decided we would discard our shirts for a few minutes each day, until our skins became accustomed to the heat. We finally turned a dark yellowish-brown, which didn't harm us. We walked in public with only our trousers and hats. Some dubbed us as the Mutt and Jeff Indians.

New Haven city was relatively free from crime. The relationship between the different ethnic communities seemed very good. Sex was discussed by men on the job. Peddlers selling ice-cream also sold condoms on the side. Some said brothels existed in New Haven. In American slang they were called 'Cat Houses'. I never had evidence such was the case. Some Americans had a superstition that if you were down on your luck, you should make love to a coloured woman.

Work on the railroad was reduced to three days a week. Lay-offs became the order of the day. As the depression grew worse, the real recession started to take effect. The workers had no protection, no social welfare benefit. The factories simply shut down. The mill owners took to their yachts and sailed south. The Salvation Army and city charities opened soup kitchens. During a short stay in New York, I witnessed people huddle side-by-side, sleeping under store awnings and in the under-street levels of steam-heated Grand Central Station. To board a train I picked my way through rows of sleeping men, lying on sheets of newspapers on the tiled platform.

All private banking firms folded. People lost their complete life savings. I knew of Irish emigrants who were committed to a mental institution on hearing that they had become destitute in one telling blow. I was present when a young, newly married man tried to end his misery because he could no longer support his wife. Luckily, he survived in hospital. Only deposits in the Federal Reserve banks were safe. Twenty-eight million were unemployed, from Florida to the state of Maine, and from New York to the Golden Gate Bridge, San Francisco. The richest and most powerful country in the world, which held the world's greatest gold reserve, was now burning a surplus of unwanted grain – enough to feed millions – all because of a stupid trade war concerning protective tariffs on both sides of the Atlantic.

The Prohibition Act, concerning the sale of intoxicating liquor, made matters worse. The great brewing industries had to close down. Federal agents discovered several casks of Canadian beer, in with other merchandise, in our section of the freight yard. They ordered the casks to be rolled to the waterfront and borrowed our spiking hammers to burst the cask heads, before departing. Our gang salvaged several water pails of a rich golden beer. The 'noble experiment' proved to be a most ignoble piece of legislation. It bred a new breed of criminal: bootleggers, beer barons and gangsters of all vile description.

The three-days-per-week pay cheque I received, I gladly surrendered to my sister, so that I might compensate her for keeping a roof over my head, thus avoiding the bread lines, which in New York could extend for blocks. The navy recruiting office in New Haven carried the advertisement: 'Join the Navy and see the world.' Many a time I stood at the bottom of the stairs, undecided as to whether I should take the plunge or not. I consulted Paddy Reardon, my brother-in-law, on the matter. 'Take it easy Mike,' he cautioned. 'You made one mistake by coming here in hard times, don't make a hasty decision.' As the old Irish saying goes: *Léim chaorach i nduibheagan* – 'the leap of a sheep into the abyss'.

Then came a turning-point in my life, which leads me to believe that our lives are governed by some force other than our own wish. Some call it destiny, kismet or whatever. One evening when I arrived back from work, a letter from Ireland awaited me. To my surprise it contained a cheque for a considerable sum of money, from my mother, saying I could use it to take a trip home to see my father, who was not feeling well, or use the money as I pleased. I immediately took passage on the S.S. *Saint Louis* of the Hamburg American Line – the ship about which Gordon Thomas and Max Morgan wrote the true story, *Voyage of the Damned*, concerning a thousand Jews fleeing the concentration camps of Hitler, only to be refused entry to Cuba or the USA on 13th May 1939.

The S.S. *Saint Louis* was a new luxury liner. The swastika and the Hamburg American line pennants flying proudly from her masthead. Many German passengers wearing swastika emblems made no secret that Germany was gearing itself for war, and that the Third Reich would emerge victorious and become a global power under Hitler. The Irish passengers disembarked at Galway, and I made my way back to Ballinskelligs. I must admit to feeling a little crestfallen. Shattered were my grandiose dreams of starting a better life in the New World. There was a sudden realization that my mother had rescued me from the scrap heap of a jobless democracy. My whole life's ambition for betterment seemed futile, like shovelling muck against the wind. There was no use in feeling sorry for myself – why didn't I join the navy?

My father was glad to see me and I was compensated by the fact that I was with my parents in their greatest hour of need. Dad was losing ground day by day and died happily in the spring of the year. My mother implored me to leave her by herself and return to the United States. This my conscience would not allow. I would feel as if I had deserted her. Economic conditions in Ireland were at their worst, with the economic war of penal tariffs against the Irish Free State, to compensate absentee British estate owners because of arrears in rent annuities. Britain refused beef trade with Ireland. I sold two very fine bullocks for two pounds each. Calves were slaughtered at birth. If ever a case could be made for jumping out of the frying pan into the fire and back again, it could be applied to my next move. I went back to the fishing trawler and long hours of slavery.

World War Two broke out as predicted and half a million fools went flogging through hell. I was the 'kid of the drum'. 'Buddy, can you spare me a dime', was America's marching song of the surviving heroes of Roosevelt's New Deal. I was offered eighty pounds for my six acres. I declined – this was the last straw. The forces of destiny seemed pitted against my people – the Kirbys of Munster.

My mother went to her reward in 1941. She was expecting her death, and told me the day she would pass away, saying; 'I will die tomorrow with the help of God.' My parents were secure in an unquestioning faith and accepted being poor as part of their social status. I continued scraping the seabed for fish, late and early, until 1943. A local farmer's daughter, Peggy O'Sullivan, agreed with my suggestion that it is bad for man to live alone. It required a certain amount of courage, visiting her parents to ask her hand in marriage. I will always remember her father's answer: 'You're as welcome as the flowers in May.'

In those days marriage was a serious business. A letter of freedom, signed by the local canon who resided in Cahersiveen, was necessary. This freedom was given after he had scrutinized a sealed letter given to me by my pastor. Having signed the forms giving the consent of the church to the forthcoming marriage, and before sealing the envelope, he asked me how I earned my living. I answered, 'From the sea, Father – I'm a sailor.' Before I had time to explain that I was a trawler man, the good canon threw up his hands, as if in despair. 'A sailor, oh my God, go off and marry her at once and don't stay away from her too long. God bless you both, boy. God bless you.' The saintly old man probably visualized Peggy standing forlorn on some South Kerry beach, singing 'Red Sails in the Sunset'. Jack-of-all-trades and master of none, I had increased my acreage from six to twenty-six acres.

I carried out maintenance and repair work for the Board of Public Works, small farming, fishing, building a new house, storm repair on roofs, rearing a family, cutting our own peat, keeping pigs, fowl, cows and calves. In 1951 I decided I would say, 'Goodbye old ship of mine.' I divested myself of my oilskins on Ballinskelligs pier and vowed I'd be my own boss from then onwards. There is an old saying in Irish: *Is olc an chearc ná scríobann di féin*– 'It is a bad hen that can't scratch for herself.'

Peggy and myself have celebrated over sixty years of married bliss. Our family are all married and around us. We have great satisfaction in the knowledge that we can never go broke. We have our own potatoes, milk and vegetables in the garden, pork and beef in the barrel, our own hens, turkeys, and our own fuel. Perhaps I owe it all to a partner who has lived her Christian faith to the full – for better or for worse, for richer or for poorer.

## *The Isle of Skelligs*

*Beside the Isle of Skelligs*
*I cast my tapestry of twine*
*Into a dark deep*
*Mirror of stars*
*Reflecting*
*The swinging chariot*
*Of a crescent moon.*

*Each greedy mesh hung open*
*In the tide.*
*I did not reckon with*
*The serpents that abide —*
*I only wanted*
*The silver and the gold*
*Not empty meshes*
*Framed in water cold.*

*I cannot write until I mend*
*This tattered tapestry of mine.*
*Each torn mesh*
*Must be restored,*
*Then I will dip my pen*
*In waters*
*Where sunrays shine*
*And the little waves of Skelligs*
*Will whisper memories*
*In her sunlit caves.*